PRAISE FOR *BEAT THE BANK*

The Wealthy Barber *taught Canadians the importance of saving.* Beat the Bank *will teach Canadians the importance of investing well. Larry Bates makes a clear and compelling case that when it comes to our retirement savings, we Canadians are being duped. Investing for our retirements is a great idea; meekly turning over our savings to a financial advisor at a Big Six bank or other major financial institution is not. Whatever your level of financial knowledge, if you have investments in mutual funds, this book will provide the motivation, and the easy to follow directions, to help you take control of your investments and have more money in your pocket for retirement.* WANDA MORRIS, VP OF ADVOCACY, CARP

This book will pay for itself after reading chapter I. KEN KIVENKO, PRESIDENT, KENMAR ASSOCIATES, AND INVESTOR ADVOCATE

If you wonder why your bank-sold mutual funds are going nowhere, Larry Bates has the answers. He helps you leave Old Bay Street, where the advice is not in your interest, to find better investments at New Bay Street, where costs are low and consumers come first. With step-by-step instructions, Bates gives you confidence to make this journey. ELLEN ROSEMAN, *TORONTO STAR* CONSUMER COLUMNIST AND INVESTING INSTRUCTOR AT UNIVERSITY OF TORONTO'S SCHOOL OF CONTINUING EDUCATION

Enlightening, horrifying, entertaining and enormously useful. NEIL GROSS, FORMER EXECUTIVE DIRECTOR, FAIR CANADA

Larry Bates offers a detailed look at everything that's wrong with our 'traditional' investment model and, even more importantly, shows readers just how easy it is to invest their money simply... and successfully. A must read. ROBERT R. BROWN, AUTHOR OF *WEALTHING LIKE RABBITS: AN ORIGINAL AND OCCASIONALLY HILARIOUS INTRODUCTION TO THE WORLD OF PERSONAL FINANCE*

Millions of Canadian mutual fund investors unknowingly pay fees that erode their returns by as much as 50 percent over time! Industry insider Larry Bates clearly explains how, why, and what you can do about it. ROBB ENGEN, FOUNDER, BOOMER & ECHO

If it's true the best game wardens are reformed poachers, then Larry Bates' tips for beating the bank should be valuable for average Canadian investors. Bates spent thirty-five years working for the four major financial pillars and lays out three wealth builders and three wealth killers. In a nutshell he counsels investors to beat the banks at their own game by dumping high-fee mutual funds for low-cost ETFs and, for good measure, buying Canadian bank stocks. JONATHAN CHEVREAU, FOUNDER, FINANCIAL INDEPENDENCE HUB, AUTHOR OF *FINDEPENDENCE DAY*, AND CO-AUTHOR OF *VICTORY LAP RETIREMENT*

Larry shares some powerful stories over his thirty-five years as an investment banker. It's like you're a fly on the wall in his office. Beat the Bank *should be required reading in Ontario's new financial literary course in high school.* SEAN COOPER, MORTGAGE AGENT AND BESTSELLING AUTHOR OF *BURN YOUR MORTGAGE*

Beat the Bank *is an insightful, entertaining, and shocking look at how the traditional investment industry separates you from your money by design... and what you can do about it.* SANDI MARTIN, CFP, PARTNER, SPRING FINANCIAL, AND CO-AUTHOR OF *WOMEN & MONEY*

In Beat the Bank, *Larry Bates demonstrates how you can build a larger retirement nest egg by making the investment industry work for you, not against you. The book shines a bright light on issues that investors should be aware of and wary of; it's full of useful tips, insight and guidance.* ANDY AGATHANGELOU, CHIEF EXECUTIVE, TRANSPARENCY TASK FORCE

BEAT

THE

BANK

The Canadian Guide to
Simply Successful Investing

— **LARRY BATES** —

BEAT THE BANK

AUDEY PRESS

Audey Press
Toronto, Ontario
www.larrybates.ca

Cataloguing data available from Library and Archives Canada
ISBN 978-1-7753437-0-7 (paperback)
ISBN 978-1-7753437-1-4 (ebook)

Produced by Page Two
www.pagetwostrategies.com
Cover design by Peter Cocking
Interior design by Taysia Louie
Printed and bound in Canada by Friesens

18 19 20 21 22   5 4 3 2 1

Disclaimer

THIS PUBLICATION CONTAINS the opinions and ideas of the author and is designed to provide useful information and general advice regarding the subject matter covered. The views expressed are the author's alone and do not represent the views of any organization with which the author is associated. The author and the publisher are not offering individualized advice tailored to any specific portfolio or to any particular investor's needs, and are not engaged in rendering legal, tax, accounting, or other professional services in this publication. If one needs expert advice, the services of a professional should be obtained. This book is not intended to serve as the basis for any financial decision; as a recommendation of a specific financial institution or advisor; or as a recommendation or offer to purchase or sell any security. The author may hold positions in securities referred to in this book. This book solely uses historical data to discuss and illustrate underlying principles. Past results do not guarantee future performance. No warranty is made with respect to the accuracy or completeness of any information contained herein. Performance data and laws and regulations will change over time, which could change the status of the information in this book. The author and the publisher expressly disclaim any responsibility for any liability, loss, or risk, personal or otherwise, incurred as a consequence, directly or indirectly, of the use or application of any of the contents of this book.

To those who challenge the status quo
and build a better future.

Unthinking respect for authority is the greatest enemy of the truth.
ALBERT EINSTEIN

Sunlight is the best disinfectant.
LOUIS D. BRANDEIS

Contents

Introduction

MILLIONS OF CANADIAN investors are losing up to half of their retirement savings to decades of paying mutual fund fees. Most investors have no sense of the scale of this loss or its impact on their future well-being.

Are you one of these Canadian investors? *Beat the Bank* will provide the answer and much more. You will discover how the big banks and other investment providers exact this heavy toll on Canadian retirement accounts and on your investments specifically. You will get an insider's view as to how the industry convinces so many of their customers to allow it to happen.

More importantly, this book will be your guide to a better way: Simply Successful Investing. It is an alternative approach focused on the use of highly efficient, low cost investment products and services that offer the potential to double your total long-term returns compared to the use of typical mutual funds.

Your key to investing success will be learning the basics. The industry portrays investing as complex, but it can be very simple. In fact, as you will discover, the simpler the better. *Beat the Bank* will give you both the know-how and the confidence you need to put Simply Successful Investing to work for you. Your result will very likely be a more prosperous retirement and the freedom to choose an earlier retirement if you desire.

Read *Beat the Bank*. You owe it to yourself and to your family.

1

Your Best Investment

The best investment you can make
is an investment in yourself.

WARREN BUFFETT, CEO OF
BERKSHIRE HATHAWAY

A LITTLE INVESTING KNOW-HOW can go a long way. Millions of Canadians have the potential to substantially increase their retirement nest eggs, and to live better lives as a result, by getting more from their investments. *Beat the Bank* will provide the insight you need to ensure that more of your investment returns end up where they belong—in your pocket!

You'll be the judge, of course, but I believe that, among the many surprises you will discover by reading this book, the most important will be how simple it can be to invest more successfully.

Learn a bit, earn a lot. It's easy when you know how.

Mary

In early 2013 I was at my desk in the trading room on Scotiabank's sixty-eighth floor in downtown Toronto when I received a call from my sister Mary, regarding her investments. Approaching retirement and living in New Brunswick, Mary and her husband have university degrees, devoted their careers to the health care profession, raised two girls, and sacrificed to save a modest amount to supplement their pension income. The call went something like this:

> Mary: "We haven't saved a huge amount, but every dollar of it will count when we retire. We don't understand why our Scotiabank mutual fund has gained so little over the past twenty years when we constantly hear about how well the market is performing. Can you have a look?"
>
> Larry: "Sure. Let me check it out."
> (With a few clicks I found the 'Fund Facts' description of Mary's Scotiabank mutual fund.)
>
> Larry: "Mary, are you aware that Scotiabank charges fees amounting to 2.3 percent a year?"
>
> Mary: "Okay, but 2.3 percent of our gains doesn't sound like very much."
>
> Larry: "No. Not 2.3 percent of your gains. Scotiabank charges 2.3 percent of your total investment. Every year."
>
> Mary: "You mean they charge fees whether the fund goes up or down?"
>
> Larry: "Unfortunately, yes. That's the way mutual funds work. And at 2.3 percent annually for twenty years, fees have eaten up 30 or 40 percent of your money!"

I was embarrassed. I felt ashamed of my employer and of the investment business overall. (Not to pick on Scotiabank in particular; Mary would likely have experienced the same result dealing with any big bank or traditional mutual fund provider.)

Mary was shocked and upset. She felt betrayed. Mary made the mistake of unconditionally trusting her bank to treat her fairly. Instead, many thousands of dollars of her precious savings were lost.

Millions of Canadian investors are just like Mary. What about you?

Bay Street

Most of Canada's providers of investment products and services—the top banks, insurers, and mutual fund companies—are headquartered on, or very close to, Bay Street in downtown Toronto. Just as the term 'Wall Street' references the entire US financial industry, the term 'Bay Street' has come to signify the Canadian financial industry and its armies of bankers, brokers, salespeople, and advisors across the country.

There are two sides to the investment business: the 'investment banking' or capital markets business, where I spent my career focusing on large institutional investors as well as big corporations, governments, and financial institutions; and the separate retail investment business, which deals with individual investors like you and Mary. Whether you deal with a local investment advisor in Victoria, St. John's or somewhere in between, you are ultimately dealing with Bay Street.

An Enlightened Banker

I have been blessed with good fortune and opportunity in virtually every aspect of my life, including my thirty-five-year investment banking career. I predominantly worked with RBC Capital Markets, both in Toronto and in London, England, where I had exceptional colleagues and incredible learning experiences while dealing with the largest and most sophisticated investors in Canada and around the world.

Prior to joining RBC in 1987, I worked for an insurance company (Sun Life), a bank (Scotiabank), a trust company (Canada Trust), and a brokerage house (Merrill Lynch Canada). This personal tour of the 'four pillars' of the Canadian financial system gave me a unique and unusually broad range of experience to apply to my new position on the Cross Markets Desk in RBC's bond department. No, we weren't a cranky bunch. 'Cross,' in this case, referred to our mandate to create new financial products and client solutions by using various markets such as bonds, stocks, currencies, commodities, and the rapidly developing derivative products that were beginning to link them all in inventive ways. We would construct $100-million financing deals, or even billion-dollar deals with multiple components, and value them literally down to the penny. And we could quickly reverse-engineer complex deals created by others and find the best bits to add to our toolbox. Without the burden of any daily product or client responsibilities, our happy little 'financial engineering lab' was unique on Bay Street—and the timing was perfect. Sure, some ideas never took flight, but many innovations successfully delivered real value to large institutions, corporations, and governments.

The Cross Markets Desk also produced very healthy profits for RBC as innovation and value creation enabled us to charge hefty deal fees. But markets evolved, and in the early nineties the Cross Markets Desk was disbanded and we all moved on to more conventional roles within RBC. After spending a couple of years leading a team covering large institutional bond investors, I helped create—and ultimately led—RBC's Debt Capital Markets Group, which specialized in handling the rapidly increasing volume of debt financing for companies and governments, totalling hundreds of billions of dollars annually. Over many years, my team was consistently #1 in Canadian market share.

Over the past three decades, as trading volumes increased, technology advanced, transparency improved, and clients became more sophisticated, fees declined dramatically across the capital markets business. Fees paid by large institutional clients in bond and stock trading, foreign exchange, derivatives, and other wholesale products and services are now a small fraction of their former levels.

Today, RBC and the Canadian investment industry generally provide large institutional, corporate, and government clients with highly efficient, low-cost products and services. I take pride in having conceived and developed a number of innovative investment products that significantly contributed to that efficiency.

But what about the other side of the investment business: the retail market? How efficiently does Bay Street deliver products to individual investors?

Banks, brokers, insurers, and financial advisors provide individual Canadians with access to stock and bond investments largely through mutual funds and other investment products that indirectly charge fat fees. Bay Street has done everything in its power to keep both the amount, and the impact, of those investment fees secret. As a result, very few Canadians understand how much they are paying for investment products and services, or how much value they are getting in return. And very few Canadians take the time to find out. Why? There are several reasons:

- Unconditional trust in the advisor/institution
- Erroneously assuming there are no fees
- Not knowing the right questions to ask
- Fear of asking a 'dumb' question
- Not wanting to seem impolite
- Mistaken belief that the advisor/institution must act in the customer's best interest
- Disinterest
- "I just don't have time!"

In a financial system traditionally dominated by the six big Canadian banks, these institutions—and by extension the entire Canadian financial industry—occupy a position of paternalistic authority that too many individual investors respect unquestioningly, and even appreciate to some extent. The industry brilliantly capitalizes on the combination of poor understanding of fees, deep loyalty, and misplaced trust by charging Canadians the highest mutual fund fees in the world.[1] Unlike the institutional business, fees paid by the great majority of individual investors have barely budged over the years.

Bay Street fees continue to quietly strip away 50 percent or more of the lifetime investment gains of millions of Canadians. That's right, 50 percent or more!

Imagine: you work hard, you sacrifice to save, you risk your money in the market over your working lifetime, you trust your bank or advisor to treat you fairly, but their fees silently consume the majority of your investment returns. Who would sign up for this kind of treatment? Millions of unsuspecting Canadians are doing just that. And I am not just talking about inexperienced, less educated investors. Countless doctors, lawyers, accountants, teachers, successful business owners, and bankers—yes, even bankers—are in precisely this position.

What Is Fair? #1

Like all businesses, the investment industry aims to make a profit. Providing access to investments is a valuable service, and Bay Street should be paid fairly for providing it. But what is fair? It depends on what value and service you receive—but losing close to half of your lifetime investment returns to fees is not fair. It's nowhere close to fair under any circumstances. Losing 50 percent or more of your investment returns is a catastrophic failure.

The impact of investment fees on Canadian retirement accounts is more than a consumer issue, it is a major social issue of our time. Government pensions will not be nearly enough to provide a satisfactory retirement lifestyle for most Canadians, and guaranteed employer pensions are rapidly becoming a thing of the past. In order to live well in retirement, you now likely need to build significant savings and make those savings grow through investment. So, while previous generations of Canadians with guaranteed pensions could casually observe the markets from the sidelines, most of us today *must* participate directly in the markets to secure a comfortable retirement.

In other words, *you, and only you, have the burden of responsibility to get investing right.* But the structure and practices of the investment industry continue to conspire against the ability of the average investor to succeed, to maximize that retirement nest egg. This compromises not only the financial well-being of individual Canadians, but also the health of our retirement system and of our society as a whole. The good news for millions of Canadians is that the path to a more rewarding investment experience and a more prosperous retirement can be incredibly simple and easily accessible. But how do you get there?

The industry fiercely resists change, despite the tireless efforts of many: regulators have been largely ineffective, educators have not picked up the ball, and a small band of investor advocates have largely been ignored. Something different needs to be done. Louder, stronger, and more provocative voices are needed.

I had never seriously considered the damage the investment industry wreaks upon average Canadians. But that conversation with my sister Mary made it very clear and very personal. It left me determined to do something about it. As an 'enlightened banker,' I aim to be one of those provocative voices, both calling out the industry and lighting the path to better outcomes for average investors.

The Boiling Frog

If you drop a frog in a pot of boiling water, it will of course frantically try to clamber out. But if you place it gently in a pot of tepid water and turn the heat on low, it will float there quite placidly. As the water gradually heats up, the frog will sink into a tranquil stupor, exactly like one of us in a hot bath, and before long, with a smile on its face, it will unresistingly allow itself to be boiled to death. A VERSION OF THE PARABLE FROM *THE STORY OF B,* BY DANIEL QUINN[2]

What if Bay Street offered a product that made no secret of its 50 percent fees? Surely most investors would quickly make for the nearest exit. But Bay Street promotes its expensive products in soothing terms, charging only very small monthly fees or even smaller daily fees. As these seemingly tiny fees add up and compound over the years, investors simply don't notice. They take comfort in the false notion that their best interests are being served by their trusted advisor or financial institution and will unresistingly and unknowingly allow 50 percent of their investment gains to drain away.

Lucky?

I'm lucky. My advisor is an old friend. I trust him. He allows me to get into mutual funds without ever charging me a dime! AN UNSUSPECTING INVESTOR OVERHEARD IN A COFFEE SHOP

Before correcting a problem, you must first be aware the problem exists; and before pursuing any opportunity, you must be aware the opportunity exists. *Beat the Bank* makes clear both the problem of severe underperformance experienced by typical Canadian investors, as well as the potential for you to significantly boost your investment returns through an approach I call 'Simply Successful Investing.'

Simply Successful Investing

We all know there are no guarantees in life. The same rule applies to the investment world; no crystal ball can accurately predict your results, or anyone else's for that matter. But Simply Successful

Investing will give you an excellent probability of significantly increasing, and in most cases doubling, your long-term investment returns compared to the average Canadian mutual fund investor.

There are three key elements to Simply Successful Investing:

1. **Learn investment basics:** Taking the time to acquire a solid understanding of the fundamentals of investing will empower you to make better choices and achieve significantly better investment results.

2. **Think long-term:** Investments offering the potential for attractive long-term rates of return *do not* produce steady returns. All but the lowest-risk, lowest-return investments produce volatile rates of return in the short to medium term. Riding out the short-term highs and lows of the market can be stressful, but it is absolutely essential to your ultimate success. Achieving an attractive long-term rate of return on investments requires a long-term mindset.

3. **Minimize costs:** Your investment returns can be dramatically improved, not by attempting to beat the market but by minimizing costs and keeping more of your market gains for yourself, even if they are just average gains. This step alone has the potential to double the long-term investment returns of millions of Canadian mutual fund investors.

There are countless things about investing you don't need to know: this book focuses on the few things you do need to know, and it will help you gain the confidence you need to utilize the Simply Successful Investing approach. Sounds good, right? But how much time will it take? You will be astonished at how incredibly easy, carefree, and liberating Simply Successful Investing can be. It can take as little as a few hours up-front, plus a couple of hours annually. That's it! So, skip a couple of reruns of *Grey's Anatomy* or *Game of Thrones* and learn how to direct your own real-life success story with Simply Successful Investing—you might even enjoy it!

The principles of Simply Successful Investing apply regardless of your investment objective and time frame. For example, you can very effectively apply the lessons you learn from this book to saving and investing to build a down payment for your first home. But the primary focus of *Beat the Bank* is applying Simply Successful Investing to the most important, and most daunting, saving and investing challenge of your life: financing your retirement.

EVERYONE HAS A slightly different vision of retirement. Like my father, Aubrey, some dream of an early, active, and lengthy retirement. Others, like my father-in-law, Bruce, continue working well into their eighties—not because they need to, but because they love it.

What part of the vision do we all have in common? We all aim to have the *freedom to choose*. To retire or not retire, as we see fit, when we see fit, and to live a satisfying, rewarding lifestyle. If you end up working past traditional retirement age, it should be because you choose to, not because you have to. The greater your financial resources, the greater your ability to choose.

Maximizing your future financial freedom—and feeling more confident and less stressed along the way—is the focus of Simply Successful Investing.

What to Expect from This Book

Many books begin by detailing an issue or a problem and end with the solution; this book presents the solution—or at least one of the solutions—in Chapter 2. Why? To give you a sense of the potential impact of Simply Successful Investing and how easy it can be to implement. I'm hoping that when you see how, with the same initial amount invested, you have the potential to double your investment income in retirement compared to that of your friends and neighbours, you will want to know how to do it yourself.

Chapter 3 is called 'The Wealth Formula.' Don't worry, I won't make you do any math and there will be no tests! But I will explain the six powerful forces that determine the ultimate performance of every single investment you make. Understanding and learning how you can control—or can at least influence—these six forces will be the master key to your investing success.

The following two chapters, 'Old Bay Street' and 'Old Bay Street Secrets,' will give you a good understanding of how Bay Street does it; how they convince millions of Canadians to give up half their lifetime investment returns. Chances are, since you were a little kid you have been programmed to unconditionally trust our Canadian banks and other major financial institutions. You will need some serious de-programming before you can clearly see the benefits of Simply Successful Investing!

I believe these two chapters may be the most important in the book, because understanding how Bay Street operates will be the key to freeing yourself from its grip on you and your hard-earned money. By the time you finish reading, to paraphrase the brilliant rant from the 1976 movie *Network*, some of you may be 'mad as hell and not willing to take it anymore!' Put more gently, I hope you will come away from these two chapters as a much better-informed consumer with a healthy skepticism, and a 'buyer beware,' 'eyes-wide-open' attitude toward dealing with Bay Street.

Then comes the 'New Bay Street' chapter, where you will begin to discover how to *beat the bank*—how to make Bay Street work *for* you rather than *against* you, by taking advantage of one of the three methods of Simply Successful Investing:

1. Do-It-Yourself investing
2. Assemble-It-Yourself investing
3. Robo-investing

Next is a basic run through the ins and outs of stocks and bonds, with a focus on how to be a more successful, confident, and relaxed long-term investor. I then cover the basics of saving and financial planning, addressing key questions like, "How much do I need to save for retirement?" Some simple financial plans and portfolios are included to illustrate some key concepts in action and show just how easy and rewarding Simply Successful Investing can be.

Finally, I show you how to select investments that fit your plan and provide a step-by-step guide to actually making your first purchases. You'll discover how to manage your portfolio in no more than a few hours annually, by implementing the method of Simply Successful Investing you ultimately decide is right for you.

I believe that taking the time to read *Beat the Bank* and following through with Simply Successful Investing hold the promise of a more prosperous future for you and your family. I hope *Beat the Bank* makes a difference in your life.

A Step in the Right Direction

How do Canadians actually invest? There are only a few basic steps, but even experienced investors sometimes get them confused. This should help:

Step 1: If you intend to invest you must first set up an investment account (a regular 'non-registered' account or a 'registered' account such as an RRSP or TFSA) at a financial institution: a bank, credit union, caisse populaire, traditional or online brokerage firm, insurance company, mutual fund company, etc.

Step 2: If you open an investment account at a traditional or online brokerage firm, you may directly invest in stocks and bonds, or in 'intermediary' products like mutual funds or exchange traded funds (ETFs). If you open an investment account at a bank, credit union or caisse populaire branch, or through an insurer or mutual fund company, your investment choices may be restricted to mutual funds.

Step 3: If you choose mutual funds or ETFs, your funds will be invested on your behalf in a portfolio of stocks and/or bonds.

Figure 1.1: Basic Investment Steps

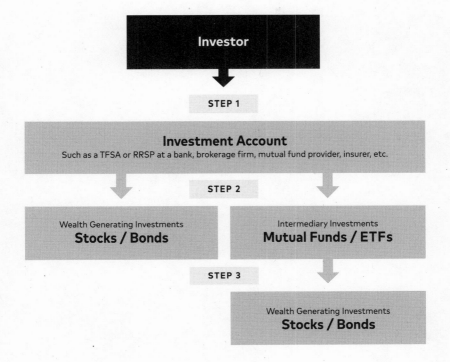

2

Double

Opportunities don't happen. You create them.

CHRIS GROSSER, ENTREPRENEUR

IMAGINE GETTING A 100-percent raise! What would it mean to you over the next twenty years? How would all that additional cash impact your life? For most of us it would mean more choice, more freedom, and more fun! And it would probably lead to less stress and increased confidence.

Your own investment experience can have exactly the same kind of life-changing impact on your future. Let's look at how the investment experiences of two thirty-five-year-old Canadian couples might compare, one following the typical Canadian investing strategy and the other implementing a Simply Successful Investing approach. (Note to forty-, fifty- and sixty-something readers: I will compare couples commencing their contrasting investment journeys in your age range, but don't skip ahead. Just trust me!)

In order to keep this simple, the couples—the Meeks and the Ables—live in a somewhat idealized world. Both couples earn similar incomes, stick to an identical savings pattern, retire at the same time and make the same assumptions about their longevity. Steady stock market returns are presumed (reflecting long-term averages), although the real-world stock market always bounces around in the short term. But these simplifications do nothing to diminish the validity or the urgent importance of this lesson. A more complex 'real-world' illustration would result in the same bottom line: compared to your friends and neighbours, many of you can likely double your retirement dollars without saving an extra cent!

Investment Jargon and Acronyms

If some of the jargon isn't crystal clear, don't worry. More detailed explanations of some of the types of investments and accounts mentioned, such as mutual funds, ETFs, TFSAs, and others, are provided in this chapter and later chapters. Just focus on the main point of this illustration: Simply Successful Investing can produce outcomes that are vastly superior to results experienced by the typical Canadian mutual fund investor. And it isn't complicated.

Thirty-Somethings

As a financial advisor for 'The Great Canadian Banking Company,' Nicole's job is to help her clients invest their savings. She invites two neighbourhood couples to a casual Friday evening dinner party, and toward the end of a very pleasant evening Nicole explains her role and talks about the importance of creating and sticking with a long-term saving and investing plan. She paints a vivid picture of the many benefits that can be achieved through a disciplined plan, and she notes the unpleasant consequences of being financially unprepared for retirement.

Neither of the couples know much about investing or picking stocks, but Nicole's logic is compelling. They recognize that ensuring their financial security in retirement will require an annual investment income to supplement their expected government pensions. Over the balance of the weekend, both the Meeks and the Ables have their own conversations and each couple decides to start saving and investing a total of $10,000 annually. By starting to save regularly for retirement in their thirties, both couples will be ahead of the game compared to many Canadians.

Let's jump ahead thirty years: both couples have diligently stuck to their $10,000 annual savings program, and in total have each saved $300,000. But what about their investment gains? Will both couples achieve similar nest eggs at age sixty-five? Not even close.

Figure 2.1: Nest Eggs at Age 65

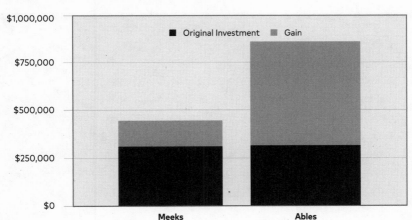

At age sixty-five, the Meeks' nest egg stands at $470,000, which comprises the total of $300,000 they contributed to their TFSAs over the previous thirty years and their net investment gains of $170,000. The sixty-five-year-old Ables have $556,000 in investment gains— more than three times the Meeks' gains—*on top of the $300,000 they originally saved*, for a total nest egg of $856,000. How is that even possible? You need to know.

Back to the beginning.

The Meeks

The Meeks feel good about beginning their journey toward a better retirement, so they set up a meeting with Nicole. By asking a number of questions, Nicole determines the Meeks have only a moderate tolerance for stock market swings. So, despite the couple's lengthy investment time frame, she recommends a portfolio that is balanced equally between stocks (more volatile) and bonds (very stable), to be adjusted annually to maintain a 50/50 split. The Meeks agree this portfolio structure matches their comfort level and their rather conservative personalities. Both open Tax-Free Savings Accounts (TFSAs) with The Great Canadian Banking Company and, following Nicole's advice, their $10,000 in annual savings is invested accordingly in stock and bond mutual funds.

TFSAs

The name 'Tax-Free Savings Account' naturally leads many Canadians to believe all TFSAs are savings accounts. Yes, some TFSAs consist of simple bank savings accounts, but they can be much more than that. As depicted in Figure 1.1 (page 15), TFSAs can act like baskets within which a wide variety of investments such as stocks, bonds, mutual funds, and ETFs may be purchased and held. These TFSAs are really tax-free 'investment' accounts. (More on TFSAs later.)

Mutual Funds

Mutual funds can be purchased and held in TFSAs, RRSP accounts, and regular investment accounts. Mutual funds hold a diverse mix of stocks and/or bonds selected by professionals on behalf of a large number of individuals. When you invest in a mutual fund you indirectly own its underlying stocks and/or bonds and, after subtracting fees, you share proportionately in the gains or losses of those stocks and/or bonds along with the other investors. (More on mutual funds later.)

Nicole does a good job hand-holding the Meeks during the major stock market slumps that inevitably occur, and with her reassurance the couple sticks with their plan. When they reach their mid-fifties, the Meeks consult with Nicole and decide a more defensive investment approach is appropriate at that stage, so they adjust their stock/bond ratio from 50/50 to one-third stocks and two-thirds bonds.

Over thirty years, The Great Canadian Banking Company's stock mutual fund performance matches the 7.0 percent stock market average annual return, before yearly fees of 2.0 percent. Meanwhile, The Great Canadian Banking Company's bond mutual fund also achieves market-average returns of 2.5 percent before fees of 1.25 percent. (If you're thinking it makes no sense to pay away half of a 2.5 percent return in fees, you're absolutely right. Stay tuned.) The Meeks don't pay much attention to fees and are satisfied with their overall investment performance. They are comfortable that their faith in Nicole and The Great Canadian Banking Company has been justly rewarded.

The Ables

The Ables totally buy into Nicole's views on the importance of saving and investing. But, rather than following Nicole's recommendation to invest in mutual funds, they decide to do some research on their own. They take the time to learn investment basics, and discover that investing can be much simpler than they expected.

The Ables discover that despite the roller-coaster ride, North American stock markets consistently produce strong gains over multi-year time periods. Given that their investment funds will remain untouched for thirty years, the Ables decide they can live with short- and medium-term stock market ups and downs if that volatility will very likely produce a better ultimate result. So they decide to place 100 percent of their annual savings in stock market funds, until their mid-fifties, when they will shift 25 percent of their portfolio to a bond fund.

Instead of investing in The Great Canadian Banking Company's expensive mutual funds through Nicole, they invest in low-cost stock and bond market index ETFs through TFSAs set up with The Great Canadian Banking Company's online discount brokerage division.

Index ETFs

Like mutual funds, index 'Exchange Traded Funds' (ETFs) can be purchased and held in TFSAS, RRSPS, and regular investment accounts. Index ETFs are professionally managed and hold a diverse mix of stocks and/or bonds on behalf of a large number of individuals. After subtracting fees, each individual index ETF holder shares proportionately in the gains or losses of the stocks or bonds in the ETF. But while mutual funds claim to pick stocks and bonds that beat average market returns (although they usually don't), index ETFs are designed to match average market returns. Index ETFs hold stocks or bonds that track the performance of major market indexes like the S&P 500 Index (representing 500 top US stocks) or the S&P/TSX 60 Index (representing 60 top Canadian stocks). Due mainly to much lower fees, index ETFs outperform the vast majority of mutual funds.

Spending a few hours per year adding to their investment knowledge helps the Ables build the understanding and the willpower they need to ignore short-term stock market peaks and valleys. They stick to their plan, spending only a few minutes a year doing a quick online transfer of their $10,000 savings to their TFSAs and, with a few clicks, adding to their ETF holdings. The index ETFs operate as designed, tracking the performance of the markets before annual fees of 0.25 percent.

In this illustration, the performance of the stock mutual funds held by the Meeks is assumed to match that of the stock index ETFs held by the Ables before fees. Likewise, the performance of the bond mutual fund held by the Meeks matches that of the bond index ETF held by the Ables before fees. The difference in the total value of their portfolios at age sixty-five is solely attributable to two factors: the difference in fees paid, and the difference in allocation between stocks and bonds.

At age sixty-five, both the Meeks and the Ables decide to retire and start drawing on their nest eggs. As mentioned earlier, with the identical savings programs, the Ables have accumulated $856,000 in savings—82 percent more than the Meeks' nest egg of $470,000.

Is that the end of the story? Will the Ables have 82 percent more investment income than the Meeks? Nope. Not even close! Because the impact of different investment choices doesn't end at retirement. At age sixty-five, the two couples are only halfway through their investment journey! What will their 'in-retirement' investment strategies be? What 'longevity' will they plan for? How much annual investment income can they safely draw down from their portfolio?

In line with their own comfort levels, at age sixty-five both couples once again reduce their exposure to stock market volatility by switching more of their portfolios from stocks to bonds. And they plan to adjust again at age seventy-five.

Table 2.1: Portion of Portfolio in Stocks

Ages	Meeks	Ables
35–54	50%	100%
55–64	33%	75%
65–74	25%	50%
75–95	0%	25%

In planning for a sustainable annual withdrawal amount, each couple assumes a thirty-year time frame for their retirement, to get them to age ninety-five, and plans to reserve a $100,000 'cushion' which may (i) cover extra expenses, (ii) fund shortfalls arising from lower than estimated investment returns, (iii) provide for further longevity, or (iv) form part of their estates.

Nicole crunches the numbers for the Meeks; she assumes that long-term investment returns remain consistent and advises the Meeks that their portfolio will sustainably provide them with $17,200 annually over the next thirty years. Using a simple online calculator, the Ables make the same investment return assumptions and determine they can sustainably draw $45,800 annually from their portfolio. (You can find links to various retirement income calculators at www.larrybates.ca.)

Figure 2.2: Annual Retirement Income from Investments

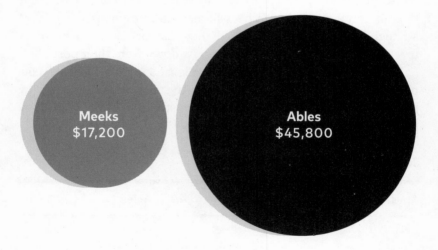

The following graph shows the total value of both couples' portfolios over their investing lifetime, assuming they make their planned annual withdrawals ($45,800 for the Ables and $17,200 for the Meeks) beginning at age sixty-five.

Figure 2.3: Total Portfolio Values: Ages 35 to 95

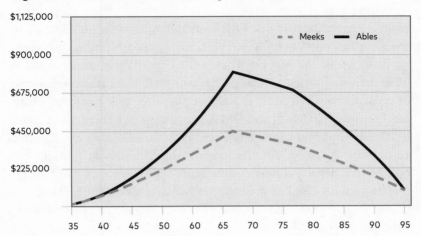

Both the Meeks and the Ables made the same sacrifices and stuck with the same long-term savings program over thirty years. But despite the same market conditions, the same longevity assumptions, and the same cushion of savings they want to keep intact in their retirement, the Ables enjoy an annual retirement income from their investments that is more than two-and-a-half times that of the Meeks.

How Did This Happen?

The Ables were not brilliant stock traders. In fact, they never picked a single stock. They did not try to chase outperforming funds. They paid no attention to day-to-day market moves and they did not listen to the daily tsunami of utterly useless media chatter about the financial markets. Over their sixty-year investment journey, the Ables employed a Simply Successful Investing approach; they took some time to learn investing basics, accepted more short-term stock market risk in return for the strong likelihood of higher long-term returns, and paid lower fees.

With an extra $28,600 annually, the Ables will have much greater freedom of choice in retirement than will the Meeks—perhaps enjoying more dinners out with friends, longer vacations, staying in their home longer, helping out with their grandchildren, and so on.

What about the Meeks? They will be fine. Their annual income from their investments during retirement will leave them well ahead of most Canadians. And, like the Ables, they will have their Canada Pension Plan (CPP) and Old Age Security (OAS) income as well. But they will never come anywhere close to affording the lifestyle enjoyed by the Ables. And they won't understand why. Just like the boiling frog, they will never quite figure it out.

What about The Great Canadian Banking Company and the rest of Bay Street? How did they make out over the sixty years of dealing with our two couples? Just fine, thank you! The Meeks paid total mutual fund fees of $217,600—an astonishing 73 percent of the original $300,000 they invested—while the Ables paid total ETF fees of just $63,900, about 21 percent of their original investment.

Figure 2.4: Total Fees Paid

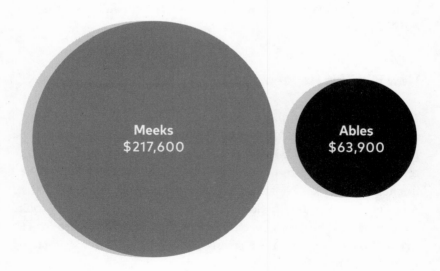

Forty-Somethings

What if, like many Canadians, the Meeks and Ables were to set off on their investment journeys later, say in their mid-forties? With a shorter time horizon to accumulate and invest their savings, what level of cash flow would they generate in retirement? Can a Simply Successful Investing approach still double the retirement income for the Ables, compared to the Meeks' traditional strategy?

Let's assume that, other than starting later than in the original example, our forty-five-year-old Meeks and Ables each follow exactly the same pattern described above:

- annual savings of $10,000 from age forty-five through age sixty-four
- the same stock/bond splits
- the same market returns
- retirement at sixty-five
- plan to live to age ninety-five with the same $100,000 cushion reserved in their savings for contingencies

The result? The Meeks' mutual fund portfolio will sustainably provide them with annual investment income of $8,500 during retirement, while the Ables' ETF portfolio produces $19,400 a year, more than double the Meeks' yearly investment income.

Fifty-Somethings

What if the Meeks and Ables begin their separate investment journeys even later, in their mid-fifties? What level of retirement cash flow would they generate with an even shorter time to save? It depends; if both couples have zero savings in their mid-fifties, they have some major catching up to do.

If you are in your mid-fifties and reading this book, hopefully you do have some savings already built up. Perhaps you own mutual funds and would like to see how a better alternative might compare. To address that scenario, let's assume both the fifty-five-year-old Meeks and Ables have already built up a TFSA nest egg of $100,000 and, from that point, follow exactly the same pattern described earlier, including the same stock/bond splits and annual savings of $10,000 from age fifty-five to sixty-four.

The result? Assuming the same investment returns as in the previous examples, and the same $100,000 cushion in reserve, the Meeks' portfolio will sustainably provide them with $7,500 annually in retirement, while the Ables' portfolio produces $15,100 a year—double the Meeks' investment income in retirement.

Sixty-Somethings

What if the Meeks and Ables do not set off on their separate investment journeys until their retirement date? If both couples have no savings when they retire, their investment income in retirement will be easy to calculate: they won't have any investment income. But let's say they both start out at age sixty-five with a $200,000 nest egg. If they follow the same pattern described above, can the Ables' portfolio sustainably produce double the Meeks' cash flow? Sorry to all you fellow sexagenarians out there, but it is too late to double. (Yes, those of us in our sixties are sexagenarians!) Still, for those of you in your sixties who may consider switching out of high-fee mutual funds, it is never too late to do much, much better than you would following typical Bay Street advice!

Assuming the same market returns, the same stock/bond splits, and the same $100,000 cushion as before, the Meeks' portfolio will sustainably provide $6,000 in retirement income annually, while the Ables' portfolio will generate $9,800—more than 60 percent ahead of the Meeks.

The following table summarizes the various outcomes for the Ables versus the Meeks, depending on when they begin their investment journeys.

Table 2.2: Meeks vs Ables Summary

Investment Income in Retirement				
Starting Age	35	45	55	65
Initial Savings	$ -	$ -	$100,000	$200,000
Years of Annual $10,000 Savings	30	20	10	0
Total Annual Savings	$300,000	$200,000	$100,000	$ -
Combined Initial and Annual Savings	$300,000	$200,000	$200,000	$200,000
Ables' Investment Income	$45,800	$19,400	$15,100	$9,800
Meeks' Investment Income	$17,200	$8,500	$7,500	$6,000
RATIO	266%	228%	201%	163%

Clearly the longer the investment time frame, the more the Ables' results diverge from the Meeks'. But even implementing the Simply Successful Investing approach in their mid-fifties can provide the Ables with double the Meeks' investment income in retirement. And significantly superior results can still be achieved by investors who implement Simply Successful Investing in their sixties or even seventies.

Of course, these are just illustrations and the amounts invested by individual Canadians (those who can save) vary widely. But, regardless of whether annual savings are lower or higher than the $10,000 round number used in the examples, *the actual real-life investment performance achieved by the great majority of Canadian investors looks a lot like the Meeks.* Why?

1. Reliance on traditional investment advisors
2. Focus on short-term risk avoidance rather than long-term growth
3. The impact of high fees

Yet like the Ables, a growing number of investors are earning higher long-term returns and keeping a much larger share of those returns by:

1. Learning investment basics
2. Thinking long-term
3. Minimizing costs

Like the Ables, my sister Mary found a better way. You can, too.

3

The Wealth Formula

Maximize Wealth Builders.
Minimize Wealth Killers.

SIX POWERFUL FORCES will determine the sum of your future wealth: three 'Wealth Builders' and three 'Wealth Killers.' Their impact will pull you and your money in different directions, often at the same time, working either to grow or shrink your wealth. Small variations in any one of these opposing forces can have an enormous influence on your ultimate investment outcome.

Figure 3.1: Six Forces

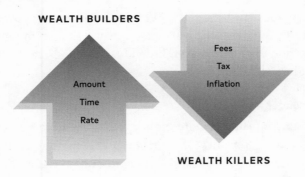

The combined effects of these six forces can be captured in one simple formula, The Wealth Formula. Understanding and managing your own Wealth Formula will be your key to Simply Successful Investing. Fear not, you don't need to crunch any numbers! Your goal here should simply be to come away from this section with a good general understanding of how the six forces will influence your ultimate investment outcome.

Figure 3.2: The Wealth Formula

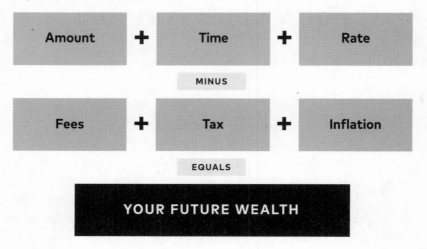

Wealth Builders

Simple, obvious, and almighty! While the astounding power of the three Wealth Builders acting in concert may at first seem implausible and take time to sink in, taken individually, each Wealth Builder is easily understandable.

Wealth Builder #1: Amount

All else being equal, the more money you save and invest, the more you end up with... right? Of course. But while it may be obvious, it isn't easy—saving is hard work! But saving and investing more today, and regularly over time, means more wealth—perhaps significantly more wealth—in the future. I will discuss saving in more detail in Chapter 10 and there will be lots more on investing wisely and efficiently in the chapters to come.

Wealth Builder #2: Time

Investing is a long-term game. Decades long. Assuming a positive rate of return on investment, the longer the time period over which you save and invest, the better. Table 3.1 demonstrates how time can have a very powerful impact on your investing results.

Let's say that you aim to achieve a $200,000 nest egg at age sixty-five, and that a 6 percent average annual rate of return on investments can be achieved. If you start at age twenty-five and save $100 monthly for forty years (for a total of $48,000), you would earn investment gains of $152,000 and have your target $200,000 nest egg at age sixty-five. Delaying your savings program until age thirty-five would require doubling your rate of monthly savings to $200 in order to achieve the same $200,000 nest egg at age sixty-five. Starting your investment plan later in life would require increasingly greater rates of saving, as well as total aggregate savings required to achieve the same $200,000 result at age sixty-five.

In other words, the sooner you start saving, the less you need to save in order to achieve the same ultimate result.

Table 3.1: Savings Required to Reach $200,000 at Age 65 (assuming 6 percent annual returns)

Starting Age	Monthly Savings	Aggregate Savings	Investment Gains	Age 65 Nest Egg
25	$100	$48,000	$152,000	$200,000
35	$200	$72,000	$128,000	$200,000
45	$433	$103,920	$96,080	$200,000
55	$1,220	$146,400	$53,600	$200,000

Wealth Builder #3: Rate

Okay, another obvious point: the higher the rate of return on your investments, the better your result. How might you earn an attractive rate of return on your investments? I will touch on that shortly and fully address this challenge in later chapters.

That's it: really simple. Each of these three Wealth Builders will individually have a significant positive influence on your ultimate investment outcome. But here is the really cool bit. The combined impact of Amount, Time, and Rate can produce astonishing results!

Magic

What did Albert Einstein call the most powerful force in the universe? Nuclear energy? No. The speed of light? Not even close. Your best friend's chili recipe? Never!

The most powerful force in the universe is compound interest. ALBERT EINSTEIN

Let me explain how compounding magic is created.

If you invest $100 with an annual 6 percent return, and the total of $106 that you've accumulated at the end of one year is 're-invested' at the same rate, and you repeat that pattern of re-investing the accumulated total each year, your initial investment of $100 produces a value of $179 after ten years. ('Re-investment' means immediately investing any amount received on your investments, such as interest or dividend payments, rather than cashing in any of what you've earned.)

The total $79 gain over ten years comprises $60 of 'simple' return on the original $100 (ten years of 6 percent return on $100) plus an additional $19 earned through compounding. How is this extra $19 generated? Because after one year, you are earning 6 percent, not just on the original $100, but on $106—your original $100 plus the $6 you earned in year one. So in year two you earn a little more than $6, and in year three you earn a little more again, and so on. In every subsequent year, you earn increasingly larger amounts.

In years eleven to twenty you earn another $60 of simple return on the original $100 investment (another ten years of 6 percent returns), but you also earn an additional $82 through compounding. In the third decade, you earn another $60 on the original amount, plus another $194 through compounding. After forty years, you have your original $100 investment, plus $240 in simple return and a compounding return of $689, for a total value of $929! Now that is magic! It's the magic of amount, time, and rate all working in concert to build wealth.

And the magic becomes even more powerful if you can realize a higher rate of return. Look at the results for different rates of return for different periods. Fuelled by re-investment, the combination of longer time periods and higher rates of return produces incredible outcomes.

Table 3.2: The Magic of Compounding

Gain on $100 Investment

Years	Compound Rate of Return				
	0%	3%	6%	9%	12%
10	$ -	$34	$79	$137	$211
20	$ -	$81	$221	$460	$865
30	$ -	$143	$474	$1,227	$2,896
40	$ -	$226	$929	$3,041	$9,205
50	$ -	$338	$1,742	$7,336	$28,800

"Okay," you say, "I have some control over amount and time, but how do I get a good rate to create some compounding magic of my own?" Good question. Later in this book, I'll explain in detail how you can create the opportunity to earn an attractive rate of return on your investments, but here is a little taster.

In the early 1980s, fixed income investments like Guaranteed Investment Certificates (GICs) and government bonds were wealth-building titans with annual yields of 10–15 percent. That's right, you could lock in a guaranteed fixed return of up to 15 percent annually for five or ten years. But current GIC and government bond yields are pathetically meagre. A five-year GIC might provide a 2.25 percent rate of return,* while a five-year Government of Canada bond may yield even less. While highly effective in protecting wealth, *these fixed income investments are currently useless at building wealth.*

In order to achieve a rate of return sufficient to build wealth today, you must be a business 'owner.' If you have the resources, skill, desire, time, and energy required, you could start a business, or you could invest in rental property. But, frankly, most of us do not. That leaves the stock market.

Owning stocks (fractional shares of ownership in large businesses) requires zero ongoing effort. You can pay close attention to the progress of the business and stock price, or you may buy a stock and forget it for years. The company's performance and the stock price will not be influenced either way. As a stockholder, you are a business owner without the normal ongoing obligations and pressures of an active business owner, but you retain all of the potential financial benefits of ownership. Brilliant!

The stock market has produced tremendous returns over the years. I will explore the myths and realities of the stock market in greater detail later but, suffice to say for now, the potential for you to power your own Wealth Formula by harnessing stock market magic continues. Here are some examples:

As of April 1, 2018, this table shows the value of $10,000 invested in these major Canadian stocks over the previous five, ten, and fifteen years.

---

* Unless otherwise noted, all market statistics in this book are as of April 2018.

Table 3.3: Selected Stock Gains[1]

Value of $10,000	Years Invested		
	5	10	15
Royal Bank (RY)	$19,717	$30,417	$60,822
TD Bank (TD)	$20,932	$32,839	$75,034
Bell Canada (BCE)	$14,981	$25,954	$40,481
Rogers (RCI.B)	$13,805	$21,256	$108,612
Suncor (SU)	$16,690	$11,057	$43,633
Canadian Tire (CTC.A)	$24,427	$26,128	$59,863
Brookfield (BAM.A)	$22,587	$32,318	$77,632

For example, looking back from April 1, 2018, if you had invested in RBC stock five years prior, on April 1, 2013, and reinvested the dividends you received, your $10,000 five-year investment would have been worth $19,717. That $9,717 gain represents a total return over five years of 97 percent. Not too shabby!

If you had invested the $10,000 ten years prior, on April 1, 2008, your original $10,000 of RBC stock would have been worth $30,417 on April 1, 2018. Nice! A fifteen-year investment in RBC beginning on April 1, 2003, would have generated a value of $60,822, more than six times the original investment! Amazing! Where else could you have plunked down ten grand, done nothing for fifteen years, and gained six times your money?

Dividends

Dividends are payments to shareholders that usually represent a portion of company profits, and are typically made quarterly. Over time, as company profits grow, dividend payments may increase. Dividends can be taken as cash or re-invested in more shares of the same company.

If you think that's pretty good, how about this:

What amount would you have today if you had invested $10,000 in TD Bank shares forty years ago and had reinvested all the dividends over that time? Two hundred thousand dollars? Half a million dollars? A million dollars? No.

Using April 1, 1978, as a start date and April 1, 2018, as an end date, your $10,000 investment in TD stock would be worth $4,291,250.[2] *Seriously*. Forty years may seem like a long time but, given many of us will live into our nineties, it is a quite reasonable investment horizon for a thirty-five-year-old or a forty-five-year-old.

What impact did the stock market crashes in 1979, 1987, 1997, 2001, and 2008 have on the ultimate performance of this TD Bank stock? Zero. And what about those breathless hourly reports, endless stock quotes, and mind-numbing prognostications from so-called 'market experts' day after day? What was the sum total impact of all that *noise* on the ultimate performance of TD stock? Zero. That is why the following chart has only two data points. The only two investment values that really matter are the amount you pay on purchase, and the amount you receive on sale. The thousands of data points in between ultimately mean nothing. As discussed in more detail in later chapters, learning to ignore all these thousands of data points is key to Simply Successful Investing.

Figure 3.3: TD Bank Stock: Growth over Forty Years

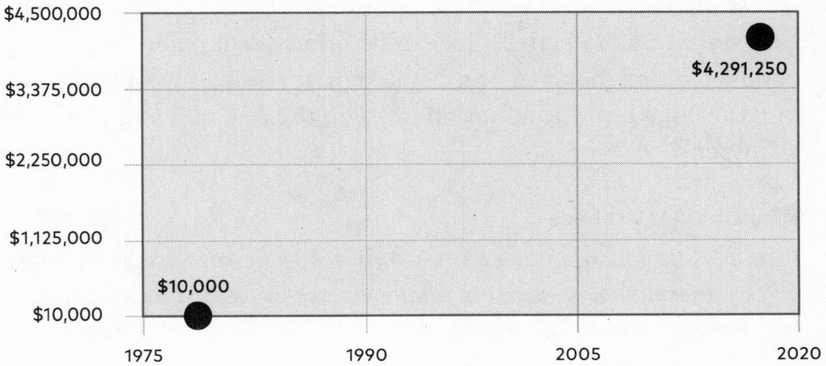

How did these and other stocks produce ever-accelerating returns over long periods of time? Ask Einstein!

These examples demonstrate that the combination of the three Wealth Builders, powered by the magic of compounding, can produce incredible wealth. While markets will always be volatile, I have no doubt that, over time, stocks will continue to produce tremendous wealth for long-term investors.

But only the positive half of The Wealth Formula has been addressed—danger lurks!

Wealth Killers

He who understands compound interest, earns it . . . he who doesn't, pays it. ALBERT EINSTEIN

While individual Wealth Builders are relatively simple and obvious, each Wealth Killer requires a little more discussion and explanation. Wealth Killers are complex, insidious, and often concealed—and they do more than just offset the benefit of Wealth Builders. Wealth Killers destroy the magic of compounding.

Reducing the impact of Wealth Killers or, where possible, eliminating them altogether is fundamental to Simply Successful Investing. Fortunately you have options, and some solutions can be very simple and effective! Tax can be minimized, deferred, or even eliminated. Inflation can be mitigated by achieving investment rates of return that beat the annual increase in the cost of living. But what about fees?

Wealth Killer #1: Fees

FEE, n. A tiny word with a teeny sound, which nevertheless is the single biggest determinant of success or failure for most investors. JASON ZWEIG, THE DEVIL'S FINANCIAL DICTIONARY

Often only partially disclosed, not disclosed at all, or simply buried deep in the fine print, investment fees are stealth wealth killers. Bit by bit, millions of Canadians are forfeiting a massive chunk of their precious retirement to Bay Street. And like the boiling frog, most are blissfully unaware.

Are you one of these Canadians? No? Are you sure?

Continued media commentary, regulatory initiatives, investor advocacy, and promotional efforts by newer, lower-fee investment providers are slowly leading to increased understanding of the scale and impact of investment fees. But overall awareness remains low.

According to a July 2016 survey of Canadian investors carried out on behalf of Tangerine Bank,[3] *"36 per cent of those surveyed claimed they don't pay any fees, and another 11 per cent were unsure if they pay fees."* Of the remaining 53 percent who knew they were paying fees, how many knew the full amount of those fees? Not many. And among those few investors who actually knew the full amount of fees they were paying, how many understood the true impact of those fees on their returns over time? Very few.

The *Beat the Bank* Three Rules of Fees

1. Find fees
2. Reduce fees
3. Repeat steps 1 and 2

Here's a simplified example of the damage high fees can inflict on the value of your portfolio over time:

Let's say you place some money in a mutual fund and instruct your investment provider to re-invest all gains. To keep the math simple, assume you invest $100. Before fees, the investments in your fund on average earn 6 percent per year, every year. (If this is all sounding familiar so far, it's because these assumptions are similar to those used in the Wealth Builders examples, but with very different results after accounting for the impact of fees.)

As shown in Table 3.2 on page 35, a compounded 6 percent return on $100 produces a total gain of $79 over ten years, a $221 gain over twenty years and a stunning $1,742 gain after fifty years. And you still have your original $100.

But let's say your advisor, banker, mutual fund provider, broker, insurer, or other financial intermediary clips off fees amounting to 2 percent of your total investment every single year. That may not sound like much but, as my sister Mary learned, these fees apply year after year, whether the value of your investments goes up or down.

So, $2 is deducted from your $6 return in the first year, leaving you with only two-thirds of your return. Your total amount invested after one year is $104 instead of $106. And it gets much, much worse, because, while the investments *inside* your fund grow at 6 percent annually, the value of the mutual fund *after* fees grows at only 4 percent annually.

The solid curve in the following graph shows the 6 percent gain over time on the investments held inside your mutual fund, increasing at a compound rate of 6 percent annually.

The dotted curve below shows your 4 percent net gain (after fees) over time on your $100 investment, increasing at a compound rate of 4 percent annually. This is your share of the gain.

The difference between the solid curve (what your investments earn) and the dotted curve (what you actually get to keep) is consumed by fees.

Figure 3.4: Investment Returns on $100 Before and After Fees

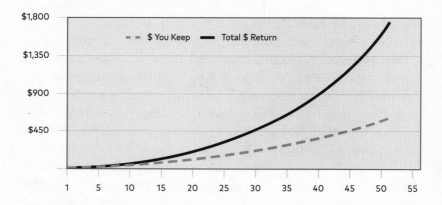

In this example, over twenty-five years your investment gains $329 before fees; but only $167, or 51 percent, of that total gain is passed on to you. Bay Street fees have stripped away $162, or 49 percent, of your return. Talk about destroying the magic! This is the power of compounding in reverse. And it keeps getting worse. Fifty-nine percent of your total return is stripped away after forty years.

Remember, this is YOUR money!

Bay Street thanks you for allowing it to strip out the majority of *your* return on *your* money that *you* have worked hard to save and that *you* have put at risk over *your* working lifetime! These numbers are hard to believe. Even I do a double take every time I look at them and I am writing the damn book!

Can you think of any other product or service you might buy with this level of fees? I can't. Maybe if you sold your house after twenty-five years of ownership but paid your realtor a commission equivalent to half of the increase in the value of your home. Would you be okay with that? I didn't think so.

Why do millions of Canadian investors sit idly by and let it happen? How does Bay Street keep so many investors comfortable, contented, and complacent in that warming pot of water? You will find the answer to that vexing question in the following chapters.

Before addressing the other two Wealth Killers, tax and inflation, let's take a closer look at how to measure fees in order to more plainly demonstrate their true impact.

T-REX Scores:
Truth and Dinosaurs

Most investment fees are quoted (if they are quoted!) as a percentage of the amount invested. So, a fund with 2 percent fees will cost you 2 percent of your total investment annually. This method of quotation is highly misleading for three reasons.

1. Fundamental to any economic transaction is a cost–benefit analysis. Whether buying a cup of coffee, a new car or a new home, or paying for a service like a carwash or high-speed internet connection, an engaged consumer compares the potential benefit offered against the price to be paid. Consciously, or probably more often subconsciously, consumers ask themselves the question, "Is the cost fair compared with the benefit offered?" There is no reason investing should be any different. The benefit you are seeking is to *earn a return on your investment*. Quoting the cost as a *percentage of that return* would provide a more accurate representation of the cost versus the benefit received. Of course, you can't accurately predict future investment returns, but you can use reasonable projections. For example, you might project a one-year total investment return of 6 percent. In this case, a fee of 2 percent of the *total amount invested* would consume 33.3 percent of the projected benefit. The same fee would consume 25 percent of an 8 percent *pre-fee* investment return. So you can conclude that, assuming a pre-fee investment return of 6 to 8 percent,

the cost of the product is somewhere between 25 to 33.3 percent of the total benefit over one year.

2. When a product will be owned for years or decades, quoting the fee as an amount owing over an arbitrary fraction of that time frame (that is, one year) makes no sense. For example, a thirty-five-year-old looking to invest for a long retirement stretching from age sixty-five to age ninety-five might use a fifty-year average investment horizon, while a couple saving to finance a newborn's post-secondary education might use a twenty-year average horizon. Quoting an annual fee doesn't tell you much about the total cost over what is typically a multi-decade investment time frame. Providing an estimate of the total fee on the basis of your projected investment horizon would be much more revealing.

3. When you pay investment fees, you lose twice. You lose the fee *and* you lose some of your compounding magic. Annual fee quotations give no indication that your 'compounding loss' accelerates as the years pass.

I have developed a much more revealing way to measure the impact of fees on your investments: simply project *how much of your total investment return you actually get to keep after fees*. This method of demonstrating the impact of investment fees, which I call the 'Total Return Efficiency Index Score' or 'T-REX Score,' addresses the three shortcomings of the conventional fee quotation.

T-REX Scores:

1. compare cost (fees) versus benefit (gain)
2. allow for a wide range of time frames
3. fully capture the ever-growing compounding loss

Your T-REX Score will tell you how efficiently the returns on your underlying investments translate into returns *for you*. The higher your T-REX Score, the more of your investment return you get to keep.

You will find the T-REX calculator at www.larrybates.ca. Assuming you know the full amount of all investment fees you are paying, it's very simple to project your score. The required inputs are:

- investment amount
- projected average annual return on underlying investments before fees
- annual fees
- projected life of investment (time horizon)

Here are some sample T-REX Scores with various time periods and annual fees, assuming the underlying investments produce an annual return of 6 percent:

Table 3.4: Sample T-REX Scores

Underlying Asset Return: 6 percent annually

	Annual Fee				
Years	0.00%	0.25%	1.00%	2.00%	3.00%
1	100%	96%	83%	67%	50%
10	100%	95%	80%	61%	43%
20	100%	93%	75%	54%	37%
30	100%	92%	70%	47%	30%
40	100%	90%	65%	41%	24%

Every investor pays fees but, just for illustrative purposes, if you were to pay no fees at all, your T-REX Score is 100 percent regardless of your time horizon.

If, like the Ables, you pay annual fees of 0.25 percent, your T-REX Score over twenty years would be 93 percent. In other words, you would keep 93 percent of your total gain, while the amount lost in fees (your 'TRUE FEE') totals 7 percent of your gain. So, the score is:

You: 93 percent
Bay Street: 7 percent

With a 1 percent annual fee, your twenty-year T-REX Score falls to 75 percent and, correspondingly, your TRUE FEE jumps to 25 percent.

An annual fee of 2 percent over twenty years produces a T-REX Score of 54 percent and a TRUE FEE of 46 percent, while the same 2 percent annual fee results in a forty-year T-REX Score of 41 percent and a TRUE FEE of 59 percent.

As you can see, the higher the annual fee and the longer the time horizon, the lower your T-REX Score (and, of course, the higher your TRUE FEE).

Very long investment time frames (which are now very realistic, given increased life expectancies) combined with high fees produce T-REX Scores well below 50 percent.

What Is Fair? #2

What is a reasonable T-REX Score? What is a fair TRUE FEE? It depends on the package of services and advice you receive. This book gives you the understanding necessary to make an informed judgement for yourself. 'Assemble-It-Yourself' (AIY) investors like the Ables can achieve T-REX Scores of 90 percent or more and, correspondingly, TRUE FEES of 10 percent or less. The fairness of any cost you incur beyond this level should be measured against the benefits you receive, including advice and convenience, beyond the investment product itself. But in my view, investors should be unwilling to accept T-REX Scores below 75 percent or so.

Your T-REX Score

Regardless of the nature of your current investments, or any new investments you may be considering—even if you are confident you know the full extent of fees you are paying—I urge you to make the following request of your investment provider:

> "I need to get a complete and clear picture of the investment fees I am, or may be, incurring. Please provide a full summary of all investment-related fees and charges that are or will be either paid to, or deducted by, you, your firm, any underlying fund manager, and any other party involved. Please provide fee details both in terms of current dollars and percentage of my total investments.
> Thank you."

Don't be satisfied until you receive and fully understand this summary!

Once you are sure you know how much you are paying in annual fees, calculate your own T-REX Score using a variety of scenarios to get a feel for how much of your investment gains you will actually get to keep. Once you know your T-REX Score and have gained a better understanding of investment basics through reading this book, you can judge whether the services you are receiving—which may include advice on investments, retirement planning, insurance, estate planning, tax, etc.—are worth the price you are paying. If you conclude that you are keeping your fair share of your returns, good for you! If not, you need to switch to Simply Successful Investing!

You can learn more about the math behind T-REX Scores at www.larrybates.ca.

Mutual Fund T-REX Scores

What happens in the fund business is that the magic of compounding returns is overwhelmed by the tyranny of compounding costs. It's a mathematical fact. JACK BOGLE, FOUNDER OF THE VANGUARD GROUP

Your T-REX Score will demonstrate just how *tyrannical* fees can be, particularly if, like the majority of Canadian investors, you invest in mutual funds.

Mutual fund managers claim their skill will result in superior investment returns over time, but stacks of academic and industry studies overwhelmingly prove otherwise. Despite this track record of underperformance, like the Meeks, millions of Canadians own mutual funds. In fact, according to the Investment Funds Institute of Canada (IFIC), as of December 2017, total Canadian mutual fund holdings amount to a staggering $1.48 trillion. IFIC reports that 86 percent of Canadians have greater confidence in mutual funds than in other financial products, such as GICs, bonds, and stocks. But do mutual fund investors know the score? Do they understand how much of their investment gains they actually get to keep? Let's check out the T-REX Scores of mutual funds offered by some of Canada's largest and most trusted financial institutions.

For purposes of making comparisons across different funds, let's use consistent time frames (twenty-five years) and pre-fee average return assumptions of 6.5 percent for stocks, 3.9 percent for bonds, and a proportionately blended return for balanced funds, which hold a mix of both stocks and bonds. These rates of return are based on Financial Planning Standards Council's (FPSC's) 2017 planning guidelines for Canadian stocks and bonds. (Given that current pre-fee yields of bond funds are in the area of 2.25 percent, assuming a 3.9 percent return on bonds is overly optimistic, but we will stick with FPSC's guidelines.)

You can easily replicate the stock and bond mutual fund T-REX Scores listed on the next page by going to www.larrybates.ca and using the calculator. Just enter the appropriate pre-fee investment return (6.5 percent for equity funds and 3.9 percent for bond funds), the annual fee as noted in the table, and use twenty-five years as the time horizon. You can, of course, determine T-REX Scores for a wide range of other return assumptions and time horizons as you wish. (Throughout the balance of this book, unless otherwise noted, T-REX Scores will be estimated using these same rates of return and time frames.)

Table 3.5: Canadian Mutual Fund T-REX Scores

Canadian Mutual Fund T-REX Scores
See 'Mutual Fund T-REX Scores' in Appendix for source detail

Selected Canadian Mutual Funds	Size (billions)	Type	Annual Fee	T-REX Score	TRUE FEE
RBC Select Conservative Portfolio	$23.00	Balanced	1.84%	49%	51%
Investors Dividend C	$17.00	Stock	2.80%	39%	61%
Fidelity Monthly Income Fund	$13.80	Balanced	2.28%	39%	61%
TD Canadian Core Plus Bond	$14.30	Bond	1.51%	50%	50%
Manulife Monthly High-Income B	$8.30	Balanced	2.29%	42%	58%
Scotia Canadian Dividend Fund A	$4.80	Stock	1.73%	58%	42%
Sentry Canadian Income Fund A	$5.00	Stock	2.34%	46%	54%
CI Signature Income & Growth A	$5.20	Balanced	2.41%	41%	59%
Mackenzie Income Fund A	$1.20	Balanced	1.89%	46%	54%
BMO SelectTrust Balanced A	$2.60	Balanced	2.50%	36%	64%
Trimark Fund A	$3.90	Stock	2.70%	40%	60%
Desjardins Enhanced Bond C	$4.20	Bond	1.70%	45%	55%
National Bank Bond Fund	$2.10	Bond	1.59%	48%	52%
Sun Life Granite Balanced A	$2.70	Balanced	2.22%	44%	56%

- Average T-REX Score: 45 percent
- Average TRUE FEE: 55 percent

Do any of these funds look familiar? Do you own these funds or other mutual funds offered by the same financial institutions or others like them? If so, you are likely paying a similar level of fees and, assuming long investment horizons, will suffer from similarly dismal T-REX Scores. Over time you will likely lose the majority of your investment return to Bay Street fees.

Freedom 55? I think not. More like 55 percent of your money is gone!

Index ETF T-REX Scores

There is a better way: Simply Successful Investing! One of the three methods of Simply Successful Investing is Assemble-It-Yourself (AIY), and investing in select index ETFs will likely provide pre-fee total returns similar to mutual funds but leave much more in your pocket with T-REX Scores in the 90s! AIY investing will be detailed in later chapters but consider this: assuming equivalent pre-fee investment returns, an index ETF with a T-REX Score of 90 percent will produce double the net gain of a mutual fund with a T-REX Score of 45 percent. **Simply by switching from high-cost mutual funds to low-cost index ETFs, millions of Canadian investors have the potential to double the investment gains they actually get to keep!**

Note that this potential doubling of returns is not based on luck or skill or dazzling performance by a genius stock trader. The potential to double your returns compared to the average Canadian mutual fund investor is driven simply by paying lower fees.

Before you make any investment, clearly understand both the total amount of fees you will be charged, and the full impact of those fees over time. Know your T-REX Score!

Wealth Killer #2: Tax

People who complain about taxes can be divided into two classes: men and women. ANONYMOUS

As we are occasionally gloomily reminded, there are only two certainties in life: death and taxes. Just like fees, taxes can severely undermine wealth building magic. And the complexity of our Canadian tax rules seems to stretch to infinity and beyond. But there are a few simple steps you can easily take to minimize the wealth-killing impact of taxes, and significantly increase the portion of your investment returns you actually get to keep. In fact, many of you can manage this whole tax thing on your own perfectly well for decades by taking one or two simple steps: invest through either, or both, TFSA and RRSP accounts. If the amounts you save for investment do not exceed your TFSA and RRSP contribution limits, you can go this route and ignore the more complex tax rules applying to investments outside these special accounts, at least for now.

TFSAs

There is a mini-miracle in the Canadian investment world: it's the Tax-Free Savings Account. And, running counter to almost everything else to do with the painfully perplexing world of tax, TFSAs are elegantly simple.

TFSAs are 'tax sheltered' accounts that can very easily be set up at financial institutions, like banks, credit unions, traditional or online brokers, life insurance companies, mutual fund companies, etc. As shown in Figure 1.1 (page 15), TFSA accounts act like baskets within which a variety of investments may be purchased, held, and sold. The range of investments available may be very broad or narrow, depending on the products offered by the provider you choose to deal with. While one arm of a major bank or other big Bay Street institution may offer a wide range of investment products, other departments of the same institution may offer a very limited range of products.

Here is the awesome bit: gains of any kind that are earned on investments held within a TFSA will never be taxed. This allows the magic of compounding to accelerate investment growth within a TFSA, free of 'tax drag' along the way. And you pay no tax when you pull money out of your TFSA. For example, if you contribute $50,000 to your TFSA account over a number of years and earn investment gains of $25,000, you can withdraw your total of $75,000 (or any part thereof) from your TFSA at any time, tax free. It is that simple. Utopia found! One Wealth Killer down and out—a huge advantage!

That being said, your ability to contribute to your TFSA is limited. If you have been a permanent resident of Canada since 2009, and turned 18 during or before 2009, your total accumulated contribution limit as of 2018 is $57,500.

From Canada Revenue Agency (CRA)[4]:

- "the annual TFSA dollar limit for the years 2009, 2010, 2011 and 2012 was $5,000
- the annual TFSA dollar limit for the years 2013 and 2014 was $5,500
- the annual TFSA dollar limit for the year 2015 was $10,000
- the annual TFSA dollar limit for the year 2016 was $5,500
- the annual TFSA dollar limit for the year 2017 is $5,500"

(CRA confirmed that the 2018 TFSA dollar limit is again $5,500.)

If you turned eighteen after 2009, your contribution limit is reduced accordingly. For example, if you turned eighteen in 2012, your limit as of 2018 is $42,500. Additional TFSA contribution room is added annually. Any amounts withdrawn from your TFSA are added back to your contribution room in the following year, which makes TFSAs ideal for saving and investing plans of any duration beyond one year.

Too many Canadians either cannot or do not save. For those who do save and invest, make sure any meaningful medium- or long-term savings not already in or earmarked for another tax-sheltered account (such as an RRSP) goes into your TFSA account up to your maximum limit. Tax-free anything is very scarce in our world today. Take full advantage!

RRSPs

Like TFSAs, Registered Retirement Savings Plans (RRSPs) are very powerful tools in limiting the wealth-killing impact of tax. Unfortunately, these beasts are much more complex, but RRSPs are more than worth the effort to understand and take advantage of!

How much can you contribute to an RRSP? It depends on your earned income. There are many rules, but CRA makes it simple by providing you with your available RRSP contribution room on your annual Notice of Assessment, which you receive after CRA reviews your annual tax return.

Amounts contributed to your RRSP account are deducted from income in your annual tax return. Reduced 'taxable' income means reduced taxes. For example, if you make a $5,000 RRSP contribution and your marginal tax rate is 40 percent, your tax bill the following spring will be reduced by $2,000. If your employer deducts tax from your paycheque, that RRSP contribution will likely bring your annual tax owing down below the amount of taxes already deducted from your paycheques. If so, all other things being equal, you will get a tax refund! Will marvels never cease?

At the Margin

Your 'marginal tax rate' represents the rate of income tax payable on your last few dollars of income. For example, if you live in Ontario and your taxable income is $90,000 you pay roughly $20,700, or 23 percent in income tax. If you earn an extra $1,000 to bring your income to

$91,000, you will pay roughly an extra $380 in tax which means your marginal tax rate is 38 percent. You get to keep only $620, or 62 percent of the extra $1,000 you earn. Ouch.

Conversely, if your taxable income were to decline by $1,000 to $89,000, your tax payable would drop by roughly $380 to $20,320.

Marginal tax rates rise in steps as taxable income rises. To estimate your marginal tax rate, check out PwC's handy Canadian 'Income Tax Calculator for Individuals' (just search "pwc tax calculator Canada").

Like a TFSA, an RRSP is a 'tax sheltered' account at a financial institution that acts as a basket within which a wide range of investments can be purchased, held, and sold at will without triggering tax. Just like a TFSA, this allows the magic of compounding to occur free of tax-drag along the way. But, unlike a TFSA, all withdrawals of funds from your RRSP (including both your original contributions and all gains) will be treated as taxable income at the time of withdrawal. Therefore, *RRSPs do not eliminate tax*. Rather, *RRSPs defer the timing of tax.*

Because RRSPs *defer* tax rather than *eliminate* it, the true value of RRSPs can be quite deceptive. You don't 'own' your RRSP free and clear. You have a partner: the Canada Revenue Agency! In return for the tax benefit you receive when contributing to an RRSP, all future RRSP withdrawals will be taxable. If the investments in your RRSP perform well, CRA will take its slice of a larger pie. So, when it comes to RRSPs, you and CRA are in it together.

For example, if your marginal tax rate when you withdraw $20,000 from your RRSP is 40 percent, you would pay $8,000 in tax on that 'income,' leaving you with net proceeds of $12,000. So in this case, $20,000 in your RRSP has the same net value as $12,000 in your TSFA.

The following table shows the RRSP and TFSA withdrawal amounts required to generate $10,000 in after-tax cash in your hands given various marginal tax rates:

Table 3.6: RRSP vs TFSA Withdrawals

Your Marginal Tax Rate	RRSP Withdrawal to Produce $10,000 After Tax	TFSA Withdrawal to Produce $10,000 After Tax
20%	$12,500	$10,000
25%	$13,333	$10,000
30%	$14,286	$10,000
35%	$15,385	$10,000
40%	$16,667	$10,000
45%	$18,182	$10,000
50%	$20,000	$10,000
55%	$22,222	$10,000

TFSAs vs RRSPs

When you come to a fork in the road, take it. YOGI BERRA, PROFESSIONAL BASEBALL PLAYER

Can't decide whether to contribute your savings to a TFSA or RRSP? You are not alone. First and foremost, it is way, way, more important to actually get your savings into either a TFSA or an RRSP than it is to make the perfect choice between the two. Too many people never act because they aren't sure which type of account would be best. Recognize that there isn't necessarily a right answer. Be decisive. Make a choice and act on it!

If the amount you have available to save in any year matches or exceeds your combined TFSA and RRSP contribution limits, your decision is easy. Max out your contributions to both. If, however, like most Canadians, your combined contribution limits exceed the amount you have to contribute, do a bit of research or get some advice. For starters, here is the quick and dirty.

TFSAs have the advantage of simplicity and can be effectively used both for shorter-term purposes, like saving for a down payment on a home, and for long-term purposes, like retirement. TFSAs will generally produce a better ultimate result versus an RRSP if your marginal tax rate at withdrawal is higher than your marginal tax rate when you contribute. TFSAs are almost always a better choice for lower-income investors (below $40,000 in annual income).

RRSPs can produce better results for higher-income earners who expect their marginal tax rate at the time of withdrawal to be lower than at the time of contribution. For example, if you contribute $10,000 to an RRSP today when your marginal tax rate is 45 percent, you will save $4,500 in tax. But if your marginal tax rate when you withdraw $10,000 is 30 percent, you will pay only $3,000 in tax.

Remember, a dollar in your RRSP is worth less than a dollar in your TFSA. There is, however, a simple way to help 'equalize' the real after-tax value of an RRSP contribution with the value of a TFSA contribution; if you can manage it, contribute your tax refund to your RRSP as well (assuming you have contribution room). For example, if you contribute $5,000 to your RRSP and a few months later receive a $1,500 tax refund, contribute this amount as well. Alternatively (again, if you can manage it and the contribution room is available) put your tax refund toward your TFSA.

(Brief overviews of other tax-sheltered accounts—Locked-In Retirement Accounts, Registered Retirement Income Funds and Registered Education Savings Plans, as well as the use of RRSPs for first-time homebuyers—are included in the appendix.)

Regular Accounts

If you invest exclusively through TFSAs, RRSPs, and other tax-sheltered accounts, you can skip this section for now if you wish. Just jump ahead to the Inflation sub-heading on page 62. If you invest through regular, non-sheltered accounts, sometimes called 'non-registered' accounts, read on. Regular investment accounts are not sheltered from tax like TFSAs and RRSPs. Within these regular, non-registered accounts, very different tax rules with different degrees of wealth-killing impact apply to different types of investment gains. Here are the regular account tax basics you need to know.

Interest earned on bank deposits, GICs, bonds, and other 'fixed income' investments is taxable when earned, at your full marginal tax rate. The same goes for dividends received from non-Canadian stocks. Let's say, for example, you own a $10,000 bond or GIC that pays 2 percent annual interest. If your marginal tax rate is 50 percent, half of the $200 you earn each year will be payable in tax, so your annual after-tax gain is just $100 or 1 percent. Just like fees, tax on interest income kills wealth in two ways: your annual return is reduced, and the net income you have to reinvest (to fuel the magic of compounding) is diminished.

What about dividends received on Canadian stocks like RBC, Bell Canada, or Enbridge? Dividend taxation is complex but, generally speaking, Canadian stock dividends are taxed less severely than interest income, so you keep a larger share of dividends received. For example, if your full marginal tax rate is 50 percent and you earn dividends of $200, or 2 percent, on a $10,000 investment in a Canadian stock, you may pay only 30 percent or $60 in tax on those dividends, leaving you with a net after-tax return of $140 or 1.4 percent on your $10,000 investment. In this example, you keep 40 percent more from your dividend income than you would from your interest income. That means more cash flow for those in retirement and more compounding magic for savers who are reinvesting. You can find the dividend tax rates that apply to you at the PwC Canadian tax calculator site mentioned earlier.

Gains on sales of investments, known as capital gains, are generally taxable at just half your normal rate—a huge advantage! For example, if you sell a stock for a gain of $10,000, you include only half that gain, or $5,000, in your taxable income. If your marginal tax rate is 50 percent, you would pay only $2,500 in tax, leaving you with a net after-tax gain of $7,500. And capital gains tax is payable only when the investment is actually sold. Another potentially significant advantage! In other words, an investment can increase in market value at a compound rate over time, increasing your wealth along the way, but you trigger no tax until you actually sell. This tax 'deferral' eliminates the wealth-killing impact of tax on compounding.

Trigger Warning

When considering switching investments within or out of regular, non-sheltered accounts—like selling a mutual fund to buy an index ETF—be mindful of the tax implications. You will be taxed on any capital gain you have accumulated. Consider the following example.

Ten years ago, using a regular, non-registered investment account, you invested $10,000 in a mutual fund. After fees, the fund has increased in value by 50 percent or $5,000. Assuming gains had not been previously taxed by CRA, one-half of your gain, or $2,500, would be taxable at the time of sale of the mutual fund. Assuming your marginal tax rate is 40 percent, you will pay $1,000 in tax on that gain (40 percent of $2,500). Therefore, your net after-tax proceeds on the sale of the mutual fund, and your net amount available for re-investment in the ETF, is $14,000, not the full $15,000 value of the investment. You would otherwise pay tax on any gains eventually, but selling an asset crystalizes the tax liability. Inside a tax-sheltered account, such as an RRSP or a TFSA, such switches are not subject to taxation.

Okay, take a few deep breaths and relax! Congratulations for persevering through this tedious subject! You deserve a butter tart or a taste of your favourite beverage. But (of course there is a *but*), I humbly request your attention on the subject of tax for just a short few minutes more! It will be worth it, I promise!

Let's take a look at an example of how, within regular, non-sheltered accounts, identical pre-tax rates of return translate into very different net after-tax gains that you actually get to keep. Remember, being aware of the fact that tax has a different degree of wealth-killing impact on different types of income is more important than thoroughly understanding all of the detailed math behind it—but the math sure makes the difference clear!

Consider three separate investment scenarios:

1. **Capital Gain Scenario:** your investment increases in market value by 4 percent annually.
2. **Dividend Scenario:** you receive annual dividends of 4 percent.
3. **Interest Scenario:** you receive annual interest payments of 4 percent (current rates available on GICs and bonds are well below 4 percent, but this is an apples-to-apples comparison).

The following table shows net after-tax gains you actually get to keep on a $10,000 investment in each of these three scenarios over different holding periods assuming (i) a 50 percent marginal tax rate, (ii) a dividend tax rate of 28 percent, (iii) zero fees, and (iv) any interest or dividend income received, *net of tax payable*, is reinvested. For comparison purposes, the second column shows the gain that you would actually realize in all three scenarios if your investment were held in a TFSA.

Table 3.7: Same Pre-Tax Gain; Very Different After-Tax Outcomes

Year	Pre-Tax Gain of All	Total After-Tax Value of Gain		
		Capital Gain	Dividend	Interest
1	$400	$300	$288	$200
2	$816	$612	$584	$404
3	$1,249	$936	$889	$612
4	$1,699	$1,274	$1,203	$824
5	$2,167	$1,625	$1,525	$1,041
10	$4,802	$3,602	$3,283	$2,190
20	$11,911	$8,933	$7,645	$4,859
30	$22,434	$16,825	$13,438	$8,114
40	$38,010	$28,508	$21,134	$12,080

A close look at this table will tell you almost everything you need to know about the wealth-killing impact of taxes on investment income in non-sheltered accounts.

Tax on capital gains is triggered only on the sale of an investment. A $400 capital gain on selling your investment after year one would leave you with $300 after tax, or 75 percent of the total pre-tax return. What about a sale after forty years? A capital gain on the sale of an investment in year forty would also leave you with a full 75 percent of the total pre-tax gain ($28,508 net gain from the total gain of $38,010). There is no additional loss because the asset continues to compound at the full 4 percent rate, unimpeded by ongoing tax. You lose 25 percent of your gain, but no more, regardless of your holding period.

Unlike capital gains, dividends are taxed when earned, even if you reinvest those dividends. A $400 dividend in year one would produce $288 after tax, or 72 percent of the total. Because $112 in tax is payable, you don't have $400 to reinvest. You have only $288. This creates an ongoing and constantly growing shortfall in the amount available to reinvest, which undermines the power of compounding. After forty years, you retain only 56 percent of your total pre-tax gain, losing 44 percent of your returns to tax. In other words, an ongoing 28 percent tax rate wipes out 44 percent of your forty-year return.

It gets worse with interest income; like dividend taxation, interest is taxable when earned. Interest income of $400 in year one would produce $200 in after-tax income, or only 50 percent of the total gain, to reinvest. Once again, this ongoing and constantly growing shortfall undermines compounding. After forty years, a 50 percent tax rate wipes out 68 percent of your return.

Figure 3.5: Gains Retained vs Lost after 40 Years

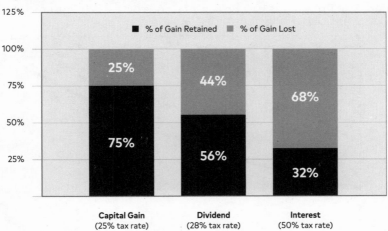

In summary, while tax rules are complex, most investors can minimize the wealth-killing impact of tax in two key ways:

1. Applying all savings first to TFSAs, RRSPs, or other tax-sheltered accounts (see appendix regarding saving through RESP accounts for children's or grandchildren's post-secondary education).

2.   Considering the after-tax impact on different types of investments held in regular non-sheltered accounts.

Wealth Killer #3: Inflation

Inflation is when you pay $15 for a $10 haircut you used to get for $5 when you had hair. SAM EWING, AUTHOR

You have no ability to influence inflation; you simply have to beat it. Consumer prices tend to go up over time. As the years pass, it takes more money to buy the same goods and services. For example, an inflation rate of 2 percent means that a year from now you will need $102 to purchase the same basket of goods you could buy today for $100. Sadly, the power of compounding applies to this Wealth Killer as well, so that after ten years of inflation you would need $122 to get the very same basket of goods. After thirty years, you would need $181 to buy that same $100 basket.

Figure 3.6: Price of a $100 Basket of Goods with 2% Inflation

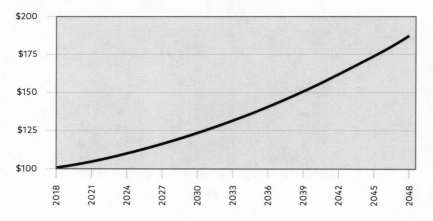

So in order to break even with 2 percent inflation, to maintain the same 'Purchasing Power' over a period of thirty years, a $100 investment today has to be worth $181 in thirty years! If you had stuffed the $100 in your mattress and pulled it out thirty years later, that $100 would buy you only 55 percent of the same basket of goods.

Figure 3.7: Purchasing Power of $100 with 2% Inflation

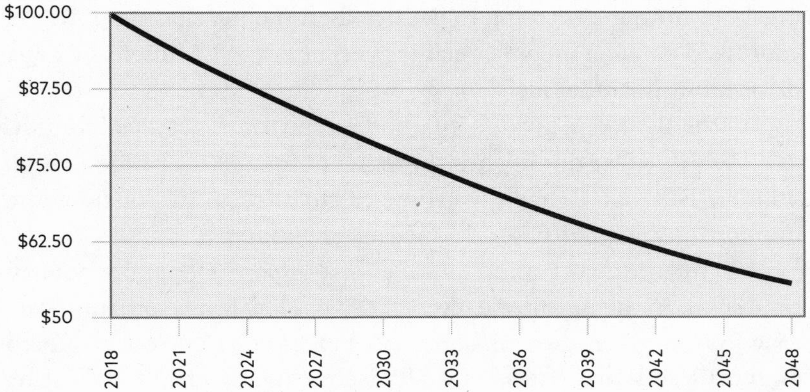

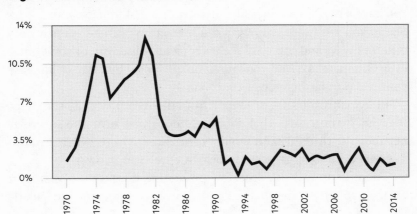

There is a very important investment lesson here. If you are standing still, you are actually moving backwards at the rate of inflation, compounded over time. *Not investing your savings is not an option.* You must invest just to have a chance to maintain the value of your money.

Averaging approximately 2 percent per year, Canadian inflation over the past couple of decades has been relatively muted. But, as you can see in the chart below, inflation in the 1970s and early 1980s was killing wealth at rates of 8–12 percent per year.

Figure 3.8: Canadian Inflation Rates[5]

Imagine having to clear an 8–12 percent return on investment, *after* fees and taxes, just to retain the purchasing power of your savings! Or, how about trying to get by when the purchasing power of your fixed pension income declines year after year. Millions of Canadians know how that feels!

Try the Bank of Canada's inflation calculator to get a feel for how this Wealth Killer diminishes the value of money over time (search online: 'Bank of Canada inflation calculator'). And consider the implications on your potential investment strategy.

Will inflation ever spiral out of control again? Hopefully not anytime soon. In the meantime, even at today's low levels, inflation isn't easy to beat given the miniscule rates of interest currently offered on most bonds and GICs. As we'll discuss in later chapters, beating inflation requires taking some risk.

The Full Picture

You now understand that your investing success will be determined by the countervailing forces of three Wealth Builders and three Wealth Killers—and the magic (or tragic) power of compounding that supercharges them.

You know that investing over long periods of time at good rates can produce astonishing results. You understand that seemingly modest annual fees can have a devastating impact on those results. You have a new way to measure and express that impact: your T-REX Score. You are aware that taxes can impact investment gains in very different ways and there are means to defer, diminish, or sometimes even eliminate tax. And you know you must beat inflation to increase your real purchasing power over time.

But what results are produced from the interplay of all six forces together? The charts that follow demonstrate how the interplay between the three Wealth Builders and three Wealth Killers can produce very different gains (or losses) in purchasing power.

There is no way of accurately predicting long-term investment returns, so the precise results of these examples are not particularly important, they are merely illustrations. The key for you is to come away from The Wealth Formula chapter with a good sense of how investment results, measured in terms of increased (or decreased) purchasing power, are impacted by changes in the six forces: amount invested, timeframe, rate of return, fees, tax, and inflation. Once you understand how the combination of these forces influences your results you will be well-positioned to begin Simply Successful Investing!

Let's compare the differences in purchasing power achieved by making a single twenty-five-year investment and reinvesting any ongoing cash received (after deducting any tax payable) given different fees, tax rates, and inflation levels. The following assumptions are applied to all the illustrations that follow.

Table 3.8: Full Picture Assumptions

	Rate of Return	Sheltered Tax Rate	Regular Account Tax Rates		
Dividends	5.0%	0.0%	10%	20%	30%
Capital Gains	5.0%	0.0%	15%	20%	25%
Interest Income	2.5%	0.0%	30%	40%	50%

The same 5 percent rate is used for the two types of stock returns in order to provide an apples-to-apples comparison. But a 5 percent return assumption can't be rationally applied to bonds when current returns are much lower, so let's assume a current real-world bond rate of return of 2.5 percent.

I use a zero-tax assumption for sheltered accounts, because (i) TFSAS are not taxed at all and (ii) an RRSP will produce the same results as a TFSA, assuming the investor's marginal tax rate is the same at the time of withdrawal as it was at the date of contribution.

Dividends

The following graph shows the changes in purchasing power under different combinations of inflation and fees, after twenty-five years, assuming you invest in a Canadian stock that doesn't change in price but pays 5 percent annual dividends:

Figure 3.9: Purchasing Power Gain/Loss: 5% Dividends

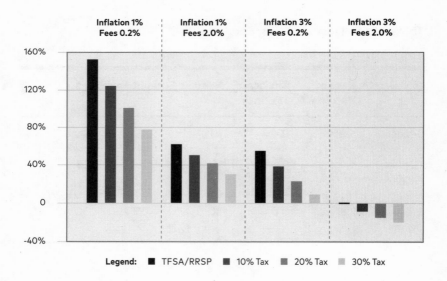

Take a look at the first cluster of four bars. They represent your purchasing power change with 1 percent inflation and 0.2 percent fees under the four different tax scenarios. As you would expect, higher taxes produce reduced purchasing power. For example, 1 percent inflation and 0.2 percent fees produce a twenty-five-year purchasing power gain of 152 percent in a tax-sheltered account (the first bar of the first cluster) while a 30 percent dividend tax would limit your purchasing power gain to 78 percent (the fourth bar of the first cluster). Of course, a similar pattern applies within each of the other three clusters as well.

By comparing the results across the four clusters, you can see the impact on purchasing power of the different inflation and fee assumptions under each tax scenario; the lower the fees, the greater the ultimate purchasing power of the investment, and of course the same goes for inflation. As you can see in the fourth cluster, a combination of 2 percent fees and 3 percent inflation would exactly offset a compound investment return of 5 percent within a tax-sheltered account, resulting in no change in purchasing power (the first bar in the fourth cluster). But paying ongoing tax on dividends in this scenario would produce actual losses in purchasing power. A 30 percent dividend tax rate would result in a 20 percent loss of purchasing power. Imagine earning a decent 5-percent return on investment over twenty-five years and ending up 20 percent behind!

Capital Gains

The following graph shows changes in purchasing power after twenty-five years assuming investment in a stock that increases in value at an annual rate of 5 percent but pays no dividends. Following a similar pattern as above, each cluster shows the changes in purchasing power with the same fee and inflation rate assumptions under four tax rate scenarios.

Figure 3.10: Purchasing Power Gain/Loss: 5% Capital Gains

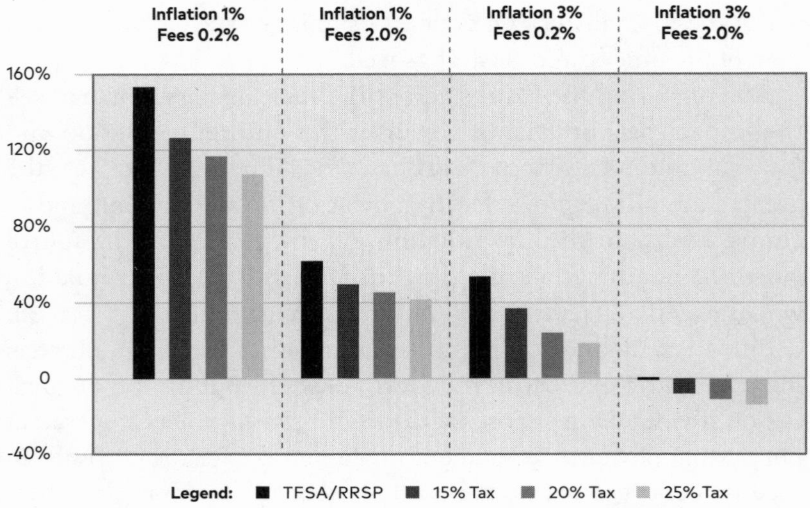

Given the same 5-percent return assumption as in the dividend illustration, purchasing power changes in the TFSA/RRSP columns of each cluster are identical to the corresponding dividend graph. The taxable capital gains scenarios generate similar patterns, but reflect different timing and rates of tax, including purchasing power losses within the 3 percent inflation, 2 percent fee cluster.

Note that despite identical 5 percent returns, as tax rates rise the differences between the dividend and capital gains purchasing power results tend to diverge, because the higher your tax rates, the greater the relative advantage of the tax deferral inherent in capital gains. The advantage of capital gains tax deferral would also be more pronounced under higher-return scenarios.

Interest Income

The following graph reveals the changes in purchasing power after twenty-five years, assuming you invest in bonds that pay interest at an annual rate of 2.5 percent.

Following a similar pattern, each cluster shows the changes in purchasing power under the same four different tax-rate scenarios, with the same inflation assumptions. 0.2 percent is still used as the lower-fee example, but now 1.4 percent is the higher-fee example, in keeping with more typical bond mutual fund fees.

These results look very different than the dividend and capital gain charts. Obviously the lower 2.5 percent return assumption is the main culprit, but higher tax rates also have a significant impact.

Figure 3.11: Purchasing Power Gain/Loss: 2.5% Interest

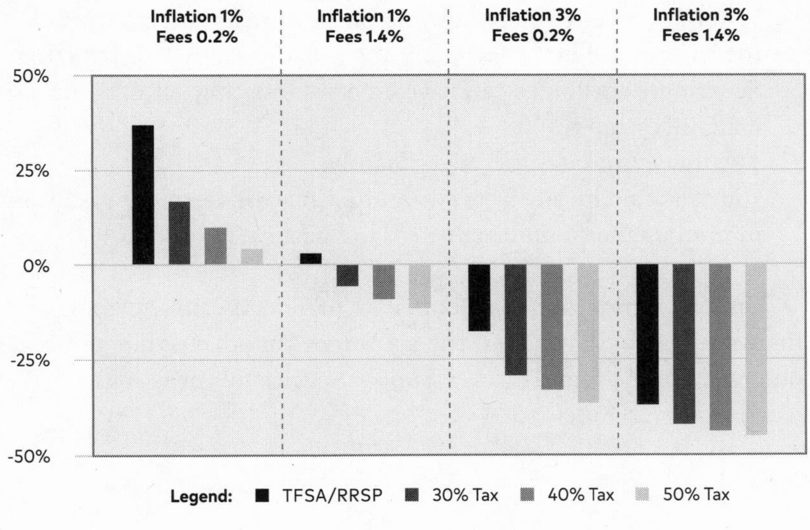

Modest purchasing power gains can be eked out in the 1-percent inflation, 0.2-percent fee scenarios (the first cluster) as well as the 1-percent inflation, 1.4-percent fee tax-sheltered scenario. But all other scenarios result in reduced purchasing power, including severe purchasing power losses in all 3-percent inflation scenarios.

This is not a pretty picture for bond investors considering today's low interest rates. Only by paying low fees, low taxes, *and* experiencing low inflation can any increase in purchasing power be achieved through long-term bond investments.

These 'full picture' results demonstrate the realities of The Wealth Formula:

- The six Wealth Formula forces will be the key determinants of your future wealth.
- Increasing your real purchasing power is the ultimate 'aim of the game'.
- Long-term compound returns can produce astonishing results over time.
- Rates of return in excess of current bond returns may be necessary to avoid loss of purchasing power.
- When it comes to claiming your share of real returns, you are at the back of the line—fees, tax, and inflation take their cuts first.
- Seemingly small fees can have a devastating impact on your ultimate investing results.
- The impact of tax varies significantly.
- You can dramatically improve your ultimate investment results by minimizing fees, limiting taxes, and beating inflation.

Understanding the basic concepts of The Wealth Formula and managing, as best you can, the six forces that drive your ultimate outcome are the foundation of Simply Successful Investing.

4

Old Bay Street

Know your enemy.

SUN TSU, *THE ART OF WAR*

I N ORDER TO invest your savings, you must deal with Bay Street. In order to reap the rewards of Simply Successful Investing, you must understand how Bay Street operates and learn how to make it work for you, not against you!

You need to learn how to *beat the bank!*

Choose One:

1. Make Bay Street Rich
2. Make Yourself Rich

Like the Meeks, most Canadian investors default to option #1. They invest through the traditional, high-cost 'Old Bay Street' establishment, including:

- investment 'specialists' at bank branches
- insurance company reps
- mutual fund salespeople
- stockbrokers
- other salespeople who call themselves 'advisors'

The vast majority of investors go this route not because they consciously choose to make Bay Street rich, but because they have been led to believe it's the only safe way to invest. It's the way their parents invested before them, and it's how their friends and family members invest today. Sadly, most don't understand the cost of investing this way, nor are they aware of other options.

But the investment industry is changing. The good news is that there is now another side of Bay Street that enables you to take advantage of Simply Successful Investing and substantially increase the investment returns you actually get to keep. Through the marriage of technology and competition, an increasing number of efficient, low-cost investment providers and products leave much more money in your pocket.

Just like the Ables, Canadians are slowly but surely migrating to 'New Bay Street' players, including online discount brokers and 'robo-advisors.' Online discount brokers offer convenient, low-cost access to stocks, bonds, and other investment products. Robo-advisors manage investment portfolios largely consisting of low-cost index ETFs tailored to individual investor needs and preferences. Although Canadians who choose lower-cost investing are a much less lucrative client base for the industry, the challenge posed by these new upstarts has actually forced many of the largest traditional Old Bay Street players to set up shop (through separate divisions, sometimes with different brand names) on New Bay Street!

If you understand how both Old Bay Street and New Bay Street operate, you will be well positioned to make the right decisions about the type of investment provider that is best for you. First let's address Old Bay Street in more detail.

The Old Bay Street Mission

There is nothing so passionate as a vested interest disguised as an intellectual conviction. FRANK HERBERT, AUTHOR

Old Bay Street understands The Wealth Formula. They get the math. They understand that quality investments can produce tremendous wealth over long periods of time.

All across this country, Old Bay Street employs thousands of investment advisors, bankers, and salespeople, many of whom are competent and well-intentioned. But Old Bay Street bosses require the vast majority of their national salesforce to offer only products with high, and often hidden, fees.

How do they do it? How does Old Bay Street convince Canadians to buy hundreds of billions in products with T-REX Scores of 50 percent or worse? (Remember, the higher your T-REX Score, the better.)

Figure 4.1: Pitch, Plan, Product, Prize

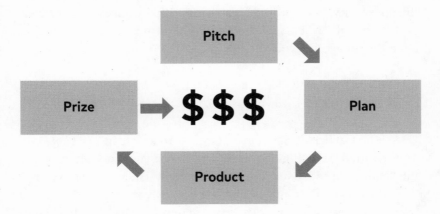

Old Bay Street employs a proven four-step system designed to use your savings to make itself rich. I call it Old Bay Street's 'Pitch, Plan, Product, Prize' strategy.

The Pitch

All the world is made of faith, and trust, and pixie dust. J. M. BARRIE,
PETER PAN

You know you need to save and invest. How do you feel about it?

- knowledgeable?
- experienced?
- confident?

Or

- bewildered?
- overwhelmed?
- fearful?

Most Canadians are in the second group, and that's just the way Old Bay Street wants it. Their relentless marketing machine plays on this insecurity, bombarding Canadians with a smokescreen of complexity, bewilderment, foreboding, and, ultimately, false salvation aimed at convincing you to:

1. *Distrust Yourself* (you are incompetent)
2. *Trust Us* (we will save you)

As Rob Carrick declared in a March 2018 article in *The Globe and Mail* entitled "The Big Six banks will fleece you—if you let them," the "banks intimidate us into a state of compliance."

Old Bay Street's 'pitch' is aimed at getting you in their door, or in some cases getting themselves inside your door. Once in, they figure to have a good shot at getting their hands on your money.

The Pitch is often illustrated in television advertisements portraying super-friendly bankers providing miraculous, instant financial solutions to extremely grateful, relieved (and usually completely witless) Canadians.

One of my favourites was the BMO 'We're Here to Help' advertisement, which portrays a small boy falling on the ice, getting smacked by a ball, requiring emergency medical attention, and running the wrong way on a soccer field as agonized parents try not to appear embarrassed. It evokes the notion that the boy represents you and your financial expertise. But BMO understands. It's ok. They will help you no matter how incompetent you may be. To see the clip, just go to YouTube and type 'BMO sports commercial' in the search field.[1] It's actually pretty funny.

Old Bay Street loves to cite an 'independent' study (which was funded by... you guessed it, Bay Street) stating that Canadians with Old Bay Street 'advisors' have bigger investment portfolios and implying that if you hire an advisor your investment portfolio will increase substantially. That's like saying that Canadians with BMWs have a higher net worth and concluding that if you buy a BMW your net worth will increase. Could it be that advisors naturally prefer to work with higher net worth Canadians so they can earn bigger fees?

For an increasing number of Canadians, however, the Pitch simply turns them off; they don't buy the 'trust Old Bay Street' marketing bit. Those who are unaware of New Bay Street alternatives often simply avoid investing. And their retirement accounts suffer significantly as a result.

The Plan

The most dangerous untruths are truths slightly distorted. GEORG C. LICHTENBERG, PHYSICIST

Old Bay Street wants to provide you with a financial plan. In fact, most Old Bay Street advisors will happily provide such a plan free of charge—seriously!

You can meet with an advisor at a bank, brokerage, credit union, or life insurance branch and get a plan completely free of any charge or obligation to do business. Some advisors would even be happy to come to your home to discuss and provide such a plan. I'm not talking about highly complex plans addressing the needs of the very wealthy—those plans will cost money—I am talking about basic plans for the 99 percent of Canadians whose circumstances and needs, while unique, are unexceptional.

If you are saving and investing for retirement, an Old Bay Street plan may include target retirement dates, nest-egg amounts, annual savings required, use of TFSAs and RRSPs, and a recommended allocation of your investments between stocks and bonds. There may be some real value in an Old Bay Street financial plan, so by all means take full advantage of Old Bay Street's offer to provide one for free!

Why would Old Bay Street 'advisors' provide this potentially valuable planning service free of charge? Simple. Old Bay Street knows that, once provided with a complimentary plan, a significant percentage of Canadians will take the next step and buy their expensive investment products because they feel an obligation to buy, they aren't confident enough to pursue alternatives, or they are unaware of the damaging impact of costs on their ultimate outcome.

Bizarrely, Old Bay Street advice most likely will exclude the single most important piece of investment advice there is: minimize costs!

Is planning 'advice' that fails to address the most predictable determinant of an investment plan's outcome—the ultimate cost of the plan—really advice? No! It is merely a sales pitch.

Don't worry about anyone on Old Bay Street preparing a plan for you without benefitting from collecting fees from you over the next few decades. The advisor—sorry, the sales rep—and his or her employer will somehow manage without you!

The Product

It is difficult to get a man to understand something when his salary depends on not understanding it. UPTON SINCLAIR JR, PULITZER PRIZE WINNING AUTHOR

After 'The Plan' comes Old Bay Street's offering of 'The Product.' Old Bay Street markets thousands of packaged investment products, which, like a perpetual middle man, *stand between you and the under-lying investments that actually produce wealth.* Old Bay Street does *not* want you to purchase stocks and bonds directly. Instead, they recommend their 'intermediary' investment products, like mutual funds, which then purchase these very same stocks and bonds but pass on to you only a fraction of the returns produced.

Citing benefits such as greater diversification, reduced risk, etc. (which can now be easily and inexpensively obtained through New Bay Street, as you shall see), Old Bay Street sales reps will relentlessly promote their high-cost, Old Bay Street products—mutual funds, principal protected notes, insurance products, and the like. Often loaded with layers of complexity, these products will be promoted as much safer and better performing than much simpler, lower-cost New Bay Street alternatives. You will likely be told that alternatives such as buying stocks and bonds directly would be extremely dangerous.

Do not mistake Old Bay Street sales pitches for objective advice!

The Prize

My investments put three kids through university. Unfortunately, they were my financial advisor's kids. ANONYMOUS

Are you richer than you think? Unlikely. Is Old Bay Street richer than you think? You know the answer! With TRUE FEES of 50 percent or more for long-term investors, Canadian mutual fund fees are among the grandest investment prizes known to humankind! At least for the companies and people who sell them. The 2015 *Global Fund Investor Experience Study* by Morningstar ranked Canada as the absolute worst among 25 countries in terms of high mutual fund fees and expenses. It is both astonishing and disturbing that Old Bay Street gets away with it.

Why do mutual fund investors never see a full annual accounting of Old Bay Street fees, let alone an indication of the long-term impact of those fees? *Old Bay Street never presents a proper bill!* Incurring high indirect investment costs by way of receiving reduced returns is just as damaging as paying high costs directly; but, because no invoice is presented, Old Bay Street never has to justify the full cost of its services. Out of sight, out of mind.

Not-So-Fine Print

A prospectus is a document meant to provide investors with 'full, true, and plain' disclosure regarding an investment product. But how easy is it to glean essential information from it? Consider Investors Group's 'Simplified Prospectus' for its mutual funds. It runs hundreds of thousands of words of dense legal language spread across 300-plus pages. Consider these statistics:

- Investors Group clients: one million plus
- Investors Group clients who have fully read through the prospectus: zero

Okay, I am just guessing on the readership count. Maybe one Investors Group client has read the full prospectus—but I doubt it! Other Bay Street prospectuses are of similar length and complexity and have similar readership counts.

Assuming blended average fees of 1.6 percent annually for the total $1.48 trillion in Canadian stock and bond mutual funds, Old Bay Street players—including the big banks, insurance companies, and fund companies—are raking in revenues in the area of $24 billion annually from Canadian investors!

The Pitch, Plan, Product, Prize strategy continues to work brilliantly for Old Bay Street. By being unclear at best or, more likely, silent on the ultimate impact of costs, Old Bay Street is telling only half the story. And millions of investors are none the wiser. You need to understand how Bay Street's fee machine works.

Bay Street Police

Why is so little done to protect Canadian investors from hidden Old Bay Street fees, misleading advertising, questionable marketing practices, and the like? First, Old Bay Street employs very well-funded and powerful industry lobby groups, which overwhelm the efforts of a small collection of poorly funded investor advocates.

Second, the primary regulators of Old Bay Street's investment dealer and mutual fund businesses are the Investment Industry Regulatory Organization of Canada (IIROC), and the Mutual Fund Dealers Association of Canada (MFDA). Both IIROC and MFDA are 'self-regulatory organizations.' In other words, these regulators are controlled by Old Bay Street. That's right, the financial industry is largely policing itself! Very often, in the battle for fair treatment of Canadian investors, the two sides are Bay Street and Bay Street. Not surprisingly, the frequent winner is—you guessed it—Bay Street!

The F Word

Canadians don't have a saving problem, they have a fee problem. RANDY CASS, CEO, NEST WEALTH

Old Bay Street generates its billions of dollars of annual revenues through a wide range of fees. Some of these fees are disclosed, but too many require effort to uncover, are buried in fine print, or are outright hidden.

Here is a summary of Old Bay Street fees:

FUND FEES

1. MERs: Mutual funds and Exchange Traded Funds charge ongoing fees, which are represented by a Management Expense Ratio (MER). You don't pay these fees directly, but they are nonetheless a cost to you. MERs are automatically and silently deducted from your investment balance, usually monthly or daily. Mutual fund MERs generally range from approximately 1 percent to 3 percent annually. For as long as you own a mutual fund, a portion of the MER may be paid as an ongoing commission to your advisor or broker.*

2. Penalties: Many mutual funds also charge 'early-withdrawal' penalties ranging from 1 percent to 6 percent of your total investment if you sell your mutual fund within five or six years of purchase.

3. Transactions costs: All funds incur costs for buying and selling securities. These costs can include trading commissions, foreign exchange costs, derivative contracts, bid-offer spreads on bonds, etc. You don't need to do an analysis of these costs. Just be aware that although they are not included in the MER, these are real costs you end up paying. Experts estimate that these additional costs range from 0.05 percent to 0.75 percent annually.

FULL-SERVICE BROKER FEES

Traditionally, brokerage firms charge commission on each stock purchase and sale. The more buying and selling, the more money the broker makes. This approach incentivizes brokers to recommend frequent stock purchases and sales! (This is usually a futile effort; see 'The Chase' in the next chapter.) While some brokers continue to utilize this transactional fee model, a growing number of brokers have switched to an 'asset management fee' model,

---

* All mutual fund and ETF MERs quoted in this book were sourced from sponsor websites as of April 2018.

which incorporates an annual fee, often around 1 percent, charged directly to clients based on a percentage of client assets.

PORTFOLIO MANAGEMENT FEES

Some Old Bay Street investment firms offer portfolio management services. In other words, they make decisions as to which stocks, bonds, and funds to hold for you. Portfolio managers charge annual fees, usually between 1 percent to 1.5 percent of your total portfolio size.

Old Bay Street brokers and advisors also take fees for selling a wide range of more complex 'structured' products, such as flow-through shares and principal-protected notes. You don't need to know exactly what these are or how they work at the moment, but you need to know the general rule of investment product fees: the more complex and fantastic sounding the product, the higher the fees. Once again, the impact of these costs is almost always undisclosed but causes real damage to the value of your portfolio over time.

5

Old Bay Street Secrets

---

*To know that someone has a secret
is to know half the secret itself.*

HENRY WARD BEECHER, SOCIAL ACTIVIST

*Transparency has the power to heal a festering sore
on the face of financial services; the festering sore of
deliberate opacity, obfuscation, and opportunism.*

ANDY AGATHANGELOU, FOUNDING CHAIR,
THE TRANSPARENCY TASK FORCE

YOU NOW RECOGNIZE that what Old Bay Street portrays as 'objective' advice can be more accurately described as a sales pitch. But to fully understand how Old Bay Street operates, to further advance your 'de-programming,' and to enable yourself to make an informed judgement about Simply Successful Investing, you need to understand the tricks of the trade. You must learn Old Bay Street's secrets!

Catch-22

Old Bay Street relies on an extremely costly and inefficient distribution system comprising tens of thousands of salespeople and their support teams across the country. In order to finance the costly infrastructure of this bloated network—and to meet relentlessly increasing quarterly profit targets—Old Bay Street *must* continue to sell high-fee products. Old Bay Street's very survival depends on it.

The majority of advisors face the same problem on an individual level; they can meet their own personal revenue targets and keep their jobs only by continuously selling high-fee products to their clients. And many are uncomfortable doing so.

As consumers, we quite often learn that the higher the cost of a product, the better it is. In other words, you get what you pay for. It turns out that in the investment world, the opposite is true. To paraphrase Jack Bogle, founder of Vanguard, one of the world's first providers of low-cost investment products, you get what you *don't* pay for. Every dollar you save in fees is a dollar that increases your total return and is available to fuel the magic of long-term compounding. In this regard, Old Bay Street's interests are not just misaligned with Canadian investors' interests—they are directly opposed to them. Such is the paradox of Old Bay Street: *The very products upon which Old Bay Street relies doom their customers to failure.* This is not the basis for a constructive relationship!

This high-fee Old Bay Street business model will eventually be wound down as Canadian investors migrate to New Bay Street in ever increasing numbers. In my view, it can't happen fast enough.

Brilliant Stock Pickers

The only function of economic forecasting is to make astrology look more respectable. JOHN KENNETH GALBRAITH, RENOWNED CANADIAN ECONOMIST

But wait! Don't the very smart, sophisticated mutual fund profession-als who forecast stock prices beat the market? Don't these Brilliant Stock Pickers (BSPs) select the winners and avoid the losers? Don't these BSPs make paying higher fees and suffering from lower T-REX Scores worth it because they produce better results?

Wrong. Wrong. Wrong.

Read 'em and Weep

How Many Mutual Funds Routinely Rout the Market? Zero. NEW YORK *TIMES* HEADLINE, MARCH 2015

Fund management performance in Canada has just hit a new low... A new report shows that the number of Canadian funds focused on US large-cap stocks that outperformed the index over the past five years was precisely zero. TIM SHUFELT, *THE GLOBE AND MAIL*, OCTOBER 2016

Ninety-nine percent of actively managed US equity funds underperform. *FINANCIAL TIMES*, OCTOBER 2016

Countless studies overwhelmingly conclude that mutual funds underperform market averages for two reasons:

1. BSPs do not consistently pick winners and, in aggregate, generate only market average returns *before fees* over time.
2. It is almost impossible to overcome the cumulative effect of—you guessed it—fees!

Of course, there are exceptions to every rule. Over short time periods there will always be some BSPs who will beat the market, but there is no known means of identifying outperforming mutual funds in advance. Research shows that BSPs with market-beating performance over two or three years will more than likely begin to underperform in short order.

"But," you may say, "I see only very impressive gains cited in mutual fund advertising. How come?"

Mutual Admiration Society

You're beautiful. Yes you are, you're very very beautiful. Extremely beautiful. ORSON WELLES, FILMMAKER

A key plank in the Old Bay Street marketing machine is its awards and ratings system. For example, Morningstar Inc., which generates the lion's share of its revenue from the investment industry, rates thousands of Canadian mutual funds with a 'star' system. Funds are divided into five categories, each represented by a number of stars ranging from one to five.

Table 5.1: The Star System[1]

Stars	Funds
5 Stars	10.0%
4 Stars	22.5%
3 Stars	35.0%
2 Stars	22.5%
1 Star	10.0%

Note that these ratings do not reflect a fund's *absolute* performance. Morningstar ratings simply reflect an assessment of *relative* performance versus other funds. So, no matter how all funds perform in aggregate, 10 percent of all funds automatically receive five-star ratings, 22.5 percent will have four stars and so on.

The largest Old Bay Street mutual fund providers operate hundreds of mutual funds at any given point in time. This means the big players will almost certainly have at least some four-star and five-star ranked funds. Unsurprisingly, these are the funds Old Bay Street promotes, while they either ditch the others or just don't mention them.

When a four- or five-star fund drops down the rating scale (which happens with great frequency), Old Bay Street simply switches their marketing budgets to mutual funds that have moved up the scale to attain four or five stars. When those mutual funds drop down the scale, the cycle is repeated.

Noting that "Investors everywhere think a 5-star rating from Morningstar means a mutual fund will be a top performer—it doesn't," an October 25, 2017, article in *The Wall Street Journal* called this practice 'The Morningstar Mirage.'

Monkey Business

A blindfolded monkey throwing darts at a newspaper's financial pages could select a portfolio that would do just as well as one carefully selected by experts. BURTON MALKIEL, *A RANDOM WALK DOWN WALL STREET*

Here is an illustration of how, despite demonstrating absolutely no collective stock-picking skill, Old Bay Street always has hot funds and star BSPs to promote.

Imagine a mutual fund provider named Simian Fundco employs eight monkeys to select stocks independently of one another. After one year, four of the monkeys have outperformed the average stock market return while four have underperformed, as one would expect with random stock selection. Of the four outperforming monkeys, two then outperform the market in year two, and of those two monkeys, one also outperforms in year three. Let's call this monkey Harriet.

In aggregate, the monkeys demonstrate absolutely zero skill. Before fees, their combined performance simply matched the market average. But Harriet's fund has demonstrated stellar performance, beating the market three straight years! Harriet is anointed as Simian's new star

BSP. Simian launches a major advertising campaign offering Canadians the chance to benefit from Harriet's proven stock-picking skill.

In the meantime, Simian Fundco has fired all four of its underperforming monkeys and shut down their crappy funds, leaving only its four winners. This enables Simian to reinforce its marketing campaign by noting that all four of its funds have outperformed the market over the past three years and that it is offering Canadians the chance to invest in four exciting new funds managed by bright, new monkeys who are benefitting from Harriet's brilliant tutelage.

Banana anyone?

The Chase

What do Old Bay Street's Brilliant Stock Pickers know about future stock and bond prices? Nothing. No one ever knows where the market is headed at any given time. If someone tells you otherwise, they are either a liar or a fool.

Old Bay Street spins the 'buy low, sell high' dream by advancing the false notion that they can recognize when a stock or fund will outperform or underperform the market. Unfortunately, most Bay Street stock recommendations are simply an extrapolation of recent performance. Stocks and funds that have recently performed well are highly recommended and vice versa. Acting on Bay Street recommendations dooms the great majority of 'buy low, sell high' dreamers to a 'buy high, sell low' nightmare. Here is an example of how the chase to 'beat' the market typically works:

1. Attracted by Simian Fundco's slick advertising campaign that focused on Harriet's stellar performance, our dream chaser buys Harriet's fund (buying high).
2. The fund underperforms the market over the next year. While this merely brings the fund's multi-year performance back to average, our dreamer has only been along for the downside of the ride. Frustrated with Harriet's lousy results and attracted to Bay Street's marketing of the exceptional performance of another,

much hotter fund, our dream chaser sells Harriet's fund (selling low) and switches to the new fund (buying high).

3. Our dream chaser continually repeats step 2, producing a constant sell low, buy high cycle.
4. Old Bay Street earns fees at each step.
5. While the market produces strong gains over time, our dream chaser gets nowhere.

Misguided

"The Misguided Beliefs of Financial Advisors,"[2] a recently released study of two 'anonymous' Canadian mutual fund dealers covering over four thousand advisors and half a million clients, finds Canadian advisors recommend investments that underperform the market by 3 percent annually. No news here. The shocking revelation is that these advisors *personally invested* the same way and suffered the same miserable results! These investment advisors appear to be earnestly recommending a course of action that they themselves follow and believe to be beneficial but that, in practice, caused serious damage. The study states the following:

"A common view of retail finance is that conflicts of interest contribute to the high cost of advice. Using detailed data on financial advisors and their clients, however, we show that most advisors invest personally just as they advise their clients. Advisors trade frequently, chase returns, prefer expensive, actively managed funds, and under diversify."

The retirement accounts of hundreds of thousands (or more likely millions) of Canadian investors are being severely damaged by what Robb Engen of boomerandecho.com calls an "army of blissfully ignorant and misguided advisors who are unknowingly giving bad advice."

Open Secrets

But don't BSPs have the inside track on stocks that are likely to outperform? These are smart, professional operators, not monkeys.

Aren't their best ideas top secret? I can only benefit from their insights by investing in their funds, right?

Wrong.

In fact, Bay Street's biggest BSPs will give you their top stock picks for free! All Canadian mutual funds and ETFs are required to publicly post documents called Fund Facts or ETF Facts, which include a list of their top ten investments. You can easily access Fund Facts documents anytime through www.sedar.com or by doing a web search combining the fund name with the words 'fund facts.' (Also, www.morningstar.ca provides a convenient 'Fund Finder' tool, which provides extensive detail on funds, including top picks.)

To illustrate, here are the top stock picks of the BSPs at RBC Canadian Dividend Fund and Renaissance Canadian Dividend Fund (sponsored by CIBC).

Table 5.2: Top Stock Picks[3]

RBC Canadian Dividend Fund Series A	Renaissance Canadian Dividend Fund (sponsored by CIBC)
MER: 1.76%	MER: 2.15%
As at December 31, 2017	As at March 31, 2018
Royal Bank of Canada*	The Toronto-Dominion Bank*
The Toronto-Dominion Bank*	Bank of Nova Scotia*
Bank of Nova Scotia*	Royal Bank of Canada*
Canadian National Railway Co*	CIBC*
Brookfield Asset Management A*	Brookfield Asset Management A*
Bank of Montreal*	Bank of Montreal*
CIBC*	Manulife Financial Corp*
Enbridge Inc*	Canadian National Railway Co*
TransCanada Corp	Enbridge Inc*
Manulife Financial Corp*	Suncor Energy Inc

*Top 10 in both Funds

It's worth noting that nine stocks (RBC, TD, BNS, CNR, Brook-field, BMO, CIBC, Enbridge, and TransCanada) are common to both top ten lists! And, of the eleven unique stocks on the combined lists, six are major financial institutions, themselves among Canada's leading mutual fund purveyors. Bay Street BSPs really, really love their own business model! The top ten stock picks of most leading mutual funds change only incrementally over time so even if the most recently available Fund Facts document is a few months old, it will likely be largely representative of current holdings. Many stocks remain top picks for years or, in some cases, decades.

In the Closet?

Canada has become the world leader in a particularly insidious form of financial malpractice... closet indexing. IAN MCGUGAN, *THE GLOBE AND MAIL*, NOVEMBER 2015

Old Bay Street BSPs justify high fees by claiming their funds contain carefully selected combinations of stocks and bonds that are quite different than, and superior to, stocks and bonds represented in market indexes and the low-cost index ETFs that track them.

But many BSPs quietly accept the reality that they can't consistently beat the market. They know that, like Simian Fundco's BSPs, they are just as likely to produce below-average results as they are to beat the market and outperform the index. They also know Canadian investors are generally a patient lot and will only sell a fund if it underperforms the market quite badly. So many Old Bay Street BSPs don't actually do much stock-picking anymore. They employ a simple strategy called 'closet indexing,' which is designed to consistently produce 'pre-fee' results that roughly match the index and 'post-fee' results that consistently fall short of the index, but not badly enough to ever get noticed. I know this strategy sounds crazy but, for Old Bay Street, closet indexing works like a charm. If you own mutual funds offered by the big banks, insurers, or fund companies, there is a good chance you own 'closet index' funds. They look a lot like index ETFs in terms of the stocks they hold, but they charge expensive mutual fund MERs. Similar product, but much higher price. Miserable result for the investor.

Here is the simple math: if you own a closet index mutual fund that carries 2.0 percent annual fees instead of a legitimate index ETF that charges 0.2 percent annually, you're losing ground at a rate of 1.8 percent annually, which can reduce your long-term investment gains by 40–50 percent. Old Bay Street closet indexers continue to bet investors either won't notice their underperformance or won't consider it bad enough to sell.

Closet index funds are purpose-built both to create wealth for Old Bay Street and, relative to easily accessible low-cost index ETFs, to destroy wealth for Canadian investors!

Salvation

Do you want a ticket to the promised land?

"Take your retirement plan off pause and hit play with a guaranteed 5 percent annual cash flow for twenty years!"

CI Financial launched their 'innovative' new G5/20 product in 2014 with an aggressive advertising campaign. And it sounded brilliant! Don't you agree? With interest rates near record lows, 5 percent guaranteed every year seems almost too good to be true.

But wait. CI didn't say they would provide a 5 percent *return on investment*. CI is only saying they will guarantee to eventually give you your money back, 5 percent at a time, over twenty years. As in, give CI $100,000 and they will guarantee to return that $100,000 back to you over the next twenty years at a rate of $5,000 a year. They are not guaranteeing a penny more.

Here is how it really works:

- CI promotes this product to advisors across Canada.
- Your advisor extols the merits of this new guaranteed product.

- You invest $100,000.
- CI pays your advisor up to 5 percent in commission.
- CI charges fees up to 2.7 percent every year for twenty years.
- CI invests your money in a mix of stocks and bonds.
- If, after paying the broker commission and taking their annual fees, the fund generates and retains a positive return, this will be paid to you.

Is CI counting on naïve seniors believing that their 'exciting' 5 percent annual cash flow guarantee actually guarantees 5 percent annual yield in addition to the return of the original investment? I don't know. But either way, CI's G5/20 program sounds to me more like twenty years of servitude than salvation!

(As of April 2018, the CI advertisements and other marketing videos were still up on YouTube. Just type 'ci g5/20' into the search field at www.youtube.com to check them out.)

There are a multitude of similar products out there variously labelled 'enhanced,' 'guaranteed,' 'strategic,' 'alternative,' 'smart,' etc. They appear to offer consumers 'salvation.' Beware. If an Old Bay Street product sounds too good to be true, it probably is; and the more fabulous it sounds, the higher the fees are likely to be.

The Dark Side

If after ten minutes at the poker table you do not know who the patsy is— you are the patsy. POKER PROVERB (ALSO ATTRIBUTED TO WARREN BUFFETT)

The questionable business practices of the 'respectable' side of Old Bay Street—big banks, brokers, mutual fund companies, insurers and other legitimate institutions—pose a more than sufficient challenge to Canadian investors. And there are always a small number of dangerously dishonest advisors within big institutions who prey on unsophisticated investors, especially seniors. But the big Bay Street players generally operate within the rules and regulations that apply to them, even if the 'Bay Street Police' tilt the rules heavily in favour of the industry.

However, there has always been a much darker side of the Canadian investment industry that operates well outside the law. In fact, Canada is recognized as a global leader in successfully concocting and marketing fraudulent schemes, which have cost unwary investors billions of dollars over the years.

Why Canada?

1. Ostensibly designed to facilitate easier fundraising for fledgling resource exploration companies, Canada's very weak securities laws and absence of will (and budget) to enforce them make Canada a breeding ground for investment industry crime. As a December 2017 *Globe and Mail* editorial declared, "Our current enforcement system is laughable and unworthy of a modern country."

2. Over the years, there have been a number of small mining and energy exploration companies that have legitimately struck it rich. This provides a thread of credibility that can be spun into tantalizing tales of deceit by other, less scrupulous operators.

3. Many of the best-known scams—such as Bre-X, YBM Magnex, Sino-Forest, and others—have been very high profile, with losses totalling many billions of dollars. But the great majority have been, and continue to be, smaller scams carried out by slick con artists who, like Leonardo DiCaprio in *The Wolf of Wall Street*, typically push 'strike it rich' gold, oil, and 'amazing new technology' stocks, priced at pennies per share, based on completely manufactured 'can't lose' stories designed to seduce unsophisticated investors.

Stay away from these penny stocks. Stay away from 'guaranteed winners,' 'can't lose' stories, and those who promote them, especially when they are associated with companies you have never heard of. Just stay away!

Duty Free?

Like most Canadians, you may naturally assume your broker, banker, or advisor has an obligation to recommend products that serve your best interests. Wrong!

Most advisors are well intentioned and, within the constraints imposed by their employers, will attempt to serve their clients' best interests but, to date, there is no legal obligation that compels them to do so. And, in any case, Old Bay Street advisors simply can't serve the best interests of their clients when the great majority of them are restricted to offering only high-fee products. Canadian investor-rights advocates are pushing for a best-interest standard while Old Bay Street is fighting tooth and nail against the imposition of any such legal duty on their advisors.

To summarize

- Old Bay Street portrays sales pitches as objective advice.
- Relative to lower cost alternatives, the investment products upon which Old Bay Street relies doom their clients to failure.
- BSPs aren't so brilliant.
- The Old Bay Street marketing machine, including its mutual fund award system, can be deceptive and misleading.
- By closet indexing, many mutual funds are purpose-built to fail.
- Canada is a global leader in investment fraud.
- Old Bay Street is fighting to avoid the legal obligation to act in your best interest.

How is your de-programming coming along? Do you see something wrong with this picture? Well, I hope so. And I hope you are open to learning how you can do something about it—to learn how to stop making Old Bay Street rich and make yourself rich instead—in other words, to *beat the bank*! The rest of this book will be your guide to doing just that.

6

New Bay Street

Freedom is realizing you have a choice.

T. F. HODGE, AUTHOR

I RECENTLY STOPPED BY a run of the mill coffee shop and bought my morning tea for $2.75 and a banana for $1.25 for a total of $4.00. I could have purchased the same banana at the convenience store across the street for $0.50 and bought a package of 100 tea bags for a cost per tea bag of $0.10, for a total cost of $0.60. Yes, I would have had to boil the water myself and supply my own container, but the tea and banana would have tasted just as good. I could have saved even more by purchasing the items at a major grocery store.

The coffee shop, the convenience store, and the grocery store each offer the same ultimate products at very different prices. It's the same in the investment world. Different types of investment providers offer access to the same ultimate products at very different prices—but on Bay Street, we aren't talking nickels and dimes!

Old Bay Street provides high-cost access to wealth-generating investments; New Bay Street provides low-cost access to the same wealth-generating investments, and is your pathway to Simply Successful Investing. If you want to significantly increase your wealth and ultimately enhance your ability to live the future you dream of, choose New Bay Street.

There are three different types of New Bay Street service providers: online discount brokers, robo-advisors, and fee-for-service advisors.

Online Discount Brokers

Several years ago, capitalizing on advances in technology, a couple of upstart 'discount' brokers appeared on Bay Street and began offering investors much less expensive access to stocks and bonds. A couple of the big banks quickly realized that they would lose a growing portion of their customers to this new business model, so they set up their own in-house discount brokerage divisions, acknowledging that it would be better to keep some of this business in house, even though it is less profitable. Today, all of the big banks operate their own discount brokerage division. For example, TD Bank operates TD Direct Investing, Scotiabank operates Scotia iTrade, and so on.

Both bank-owned and independent discount brokers (like Qtrade, Questrade, and Virtual Brokers), which all now operate primarily online, offer the same types of accounts: TFSAs, RRSPs, regular accounts, etc. And with just a few clicks they provide access to the same range of investments as traditional brokers—at a much lower cost. Most online discount brokers charge less than $10 for a stock or ETF purchase or sale, regardless of the number of shares or units you are buying or selling. For example, buying $1,000, $100,000, or even $1,000,000 worth of Bell Canada stock or an iShares index ETF through RBC Direct Investing would cost you just $9.95. Some online brokers even offer ETF trades free of charge.

Unlike traditional brokers, discount brokers do not provide advice on specific investments. However, they do offer a wide array of useful online investment information and tools, including practice accounts and tutorials. And they provide real live human support by phone or chat, covering a multitude of investment basics like how to set up new accounts; switching from an Old Bay Street provider; how to buy a stock, bond, or ETF; and more.

If, like the Ables, you can develop a good understanding of investing basics and are comfortable with selecting investments on your own, an online discount broker may be perfect for you. But many investors who could benefit tremendously from efficient, low-cost access to investments shy away from online discount brokers due to the unfortunate misconception that they are not suitable for average investors. This couldn't be further from the truth.

This false impression arises from two separate but related myths:

Myth #1: Day Traders Only

Day traders aim to make quick profits by frequently buying and selling stocks and other securities, often within the same day. (If your goal is to become a day trader, you are reading the wrong book!) Online discount brokerage firms love day traders for the obvious reason: they generate the most activity and, therefore, the greatest profitability. The discount broker marketing/advertising focus on hyperactive clients perpetuates the Old Bay Street fiction that discount brokers are not for less active, long-term investors, like you. But anyone can take advantage of the low cost and efficiency of online discount brokers, even if all you do is buy stocks, bonds, or index ETFs today and hold them for the next ten, twenty, thirty, forty, or even fifty years. No active trading required!

Myth #2: Expert Investors Only

Matthew assembles a newly purchased Ikea chest of drawers with one of those handy Allen keys. The finished product suits his needs perfectly. Is Matthew a 'Do-It-Yourself' (DIY) cabinet maker? I think not. He did not create the design, find the right trees, manufacture and precision cut the particle board, apply glues, design, and produce the metal fasteners and handles. Matthew is an 'Assemble-It-Yourself' (AIY) cabinet maker.

The label 'DIY' investor is erroneously applied to all online discount broker investors. Yes, like real cabinet makers, many investors who use online discount brokers really do it all themselves. By selecting their own stocks and bonds and determining how much and when to buy and when to sell, DIY investors avoid all MERs and other fund fees and charges. They are true DIY investors. As one of the three methods of Simply Successful Investing, DIY investing can be a highly effective and extremely low-cost approach, for those with a strong understanding of investing basics who stick to blue chip stocks and high-quality bonds. By achieving T-REX Scores of 96–99 percent, DIY investors can enjoy much higher investment returns compared to their friends and neighbours who stick to Old Bay Street products.

On the other hand, many less-experienced and less-sophisticated investors take advantage of the fee savings offered by online discount brokers to employ an extremely effective, low-cost approach without ever having to research or pick or worry about a single stock or bond. Like the Ables, they invest in—and stick to—a very small number of index ETFs that automatically select their underlying stocks and bonds for them. These are not DIY investors; they are 'Assemble-It-Yourself' (AIY) investors. A brilliantly simple strategy, AIY investing through an online discount broker, also known as 'couch potato investing,' is the lowest-cost way to automatically diversify your investments. And for millions of Canadians who take the time to learn investing basics, the AIY approach can be the ideal method of Simply Successful Investing. By achieving T-REX Scores of 90 to 95 percent, AIY investors can also enjoy significantly greater investment returns than their friends and neighbours who invest in Old Bay Street products.

In Chapter 12 I will explain step by step how you can easily build both AIY and DIY investment portfolios to produce investment gains you actually get to keep!

In order to determine whether using an online discount broker may be right for you, I highly recommend you take advantage of the practice accounts offered by most providers. This will allow you to get very familiar with the buying and selling processes before you consider doing the real thing.

Using BMO InvestorLine as an example, here are the steps required to set up an account with an online discount brokerage:

1. Go to www.bmo.com/InvestorLine and follow the prompts
2. Click 'open an account'
3. Choose 'self-directed' and select the types of accounts you wish to open (regular/RRSP/TFSA/etc.)
4. Do NOT select 'options trading' (this is for sophisticated traders only)
5. Create a password (make a note of your password and the account application number provided)
6. Enter your financial information
7. Set up the transfer of assets from your bank or other investment accounts (warning: the process of withdrawing funds from investment accounts can be very slow with some Old Bay Street institutions)
8. Print out, sign, and submit application
9. You will receive an email advising that your account is active, and that the requested initial funds transfer has been completed
10. You are ready to invest

How do you choose an online discount broker? Easy. You could simply go with the online discount brokerage service offered by your bank, but it probably makes sense to shop around—online of course.

You will find links to major online discount brokers, as well as third-party scorecards comparing the attributes of each, at www.larrybates.ca

Small Account Fees

Most online discount brokers don't charge ongoing fees for investment accounts with balances above a given level—usually somewhere between $10,000 and $25,000. Accounts below this level may be hit with an 'administration' fee of $100 annually. Even a $100 fee can represent a large percentage of a small account. For example, a $100 charge on a $5,000 account represents an annual 2 percent cost. Fortunately, there are a number of significant exceptions to this general rule that can allow small investors to avoid these fees. Some major online discount brokers don't charge ongoing administration fees for TFSA accounts of any size, while others will waive fees if you make monthly or quarterly deposits. Be sure to familiarize yourself with the small account fee policies of any online discount broker you may be considering.

Domo Arigato, Mr. Roboto

There is a major change sweeping through the investment industry, and Bay Street will never be the same. Do you want the benefits of diversified, low-cost index funds but prefer ongoing support in determining the mix of stocks and bonds that is right for you? If so and if, like most investors, your circumstances are 'unexceptional,' robo-advisors may be the ideal Simply Successful Investing method for you.

Robo-advisors automate the investment process. Go online, answer a few questions and a portfolio of high-quality, low-cost ETFs matched to your profile will be recommended to you. And the whole process is paperless—or very close to it. Once you complete your questionnaire and application, you can keep track of your portfolio performance from your laptop or smartphone.

Despite the nickname, all robo-advisors do offer email, phone, or chat access to real human expertise. Most robo-advisors do not provide comprehensive financial advice or plans, but they will discuss the suitability of your asset mix, use of TFSAs and RRSPs, evolving investment goals, and shifting preferences over time.

Several Canadian robo-advisors have launched in the past few years, including Wealthsimple (backed by the aptly named Power Financial Corporation, owner of several Old Bay Street titans including Investors Group, Great West Life, and Mackenzie Investments), Nest Wealth (backed by National Bank of Canada), Justwealth, BMO Smart-Folio, Planswell, and several others. In early 2018, RBC announced plans to launch their own robo-advisor, to be called InvestEase.

Some robo-advisors offer lower cost solutions for smaller account sizes, including accounts of just a few thousand dollars, while others offer better value for much larger accounts measured in the hundreds of thousands or millions of dollars. In addition to ETF MERs ranging from 0.10–0.30 percent, most robo-advisors tack on fees of 0.25–0.75 percent resulting in total annual fees to investors of 0.35–1.05 percent. This produces T-REX Scores in the range of 70–90 percent.

I believe robo-advisors can be the right Simply Successful Investing choice for millions of investors who are seeking the 'lowest maintenance,' most effortless solution and/or the peace of mind of having professionals oversee their ETF portfolio. Robo-advisors can also be a great starting point for investors who aren't quite ready to go the AIY route or are just starting out on their investing journey and may consider switching to AIY once they have built up some knowledge and experience.

Using Nest Wealth as an example, here are the type of steps required to set up a robo-advisor account:

1. Go to www.nestwealth.com and follow the prompts.
2. Provide your age, income, and information on any existing investments.
3. Select type of accounts.
4. Identify your investment purpose, time frame, and risk tolerance.
5. A portfolio of ETFs will be recommended to you.
6. You can choose to proceed with the recommended portfolio or request an alternative mix.
7. Provide personal and banking information.
8. Upload ID and a void cheque.
9. Input electronic signatures into account agreements.
10. Following a two- to three-day processing period, you can set up the transfer of funds from your bank account or other investment account.
11. Prior to your funds being invested, you can request a conversation with a portfolio manager, following which the original portfolio recommendation will be confirmed or adjusted based on your personal circumstances and preferences.

12. Your initial and ongoing contributions will then be automatically invested as per the final recommendation. You can speak to a portfolio manager any time you wish to consider changes.

How do you choose a robo-advisor? Once again, it is pretty easy. You will also find links to Canadian robo-advisors and third-party scorecards comparing the attributes of each at www.larrybates.ca. If you go this route, shop around. Make sure you select a robo-advisor that provides good value for the size of your portfolio.

Fee-for-Service Advisors

What if you want the efficiency and low cost offered by Simply Successful Investing through online discount brokers or robo-advisors, but also want personalized, professional financial planning advice? You may be willing to pay a fair price for the advice you need, but you may not be willing to hand over half your lifetime investment returns to Old Bay Street to get it.

Unlike traditional Old Bay Street advisors, New Bay Street 'fee-for-service' advisors aren't investment salespeople. Because they don't sell investment products, fee-for-service advisors are not influenced by investment product commissions. This enables fee-for-service advisors to provide 'conflict free' advice based on your best interests. Again, in contrast to Old Bay Street, fee-for-service advisor charges are above board. They are not deeply buried within complex products or obscured within confusing client statements. Fee-for-service advisors are paid directly by you at an agreed rate, based on the time spent or the delivery of a specific service such as providing a comprehensive financial plan.

For investors at any stage who value the benefit of professional advice, fee-for-service advisors may fit the bill. A couple in their fifties or sixties may want some advice on their target annual savings and retirement nest egg, and how their annual investment cash flows might complement expected Canada Pension Plan (CPP) and Old

Age Security (OAS) payments or other potential pension income. They may benefit from a detailed plan and ongoing advice or may only need a 'check-up' every few years. A younger investor may benefit from spending an hour or two confirming the basics of financial planning and ensuring they get started on the right foot with their savings and investing plan.

When you seek the advice of a fee-for-service advisor, you will still need to implement the investing element of your plan separately as you see fit, either through a robo-advisor or, as an AIY or DIY investor, through an online discount broker. Fee-for-service advisors range from $100–$300 an hour, and typically charge up to a few thousand dollars for a detailed plan with regular follow-up. Some offer monthly subscription options. Most fee-for-service advisors will offer an initial consultation free of charge. Adding the cost of a fee-for-service advisor to the cost of investment purchases using an online discount broker or robo-advisor can produce very high T-REX Scores for investors with substantial portfolios. For example, let's say you have a $250,000 AIY stock index ETF portfolio through a discount broker with an MER of 0.25 percent. But you want some professional advice regarding your financial plan, so you consult a fee-for-service advisor for three hours every couple of years at a total cost of $1,000 each time. This adds an average annual cost of $500 or 0.2 percent of your portfolio value. Adding this 0.2 percent expense for advice to your investment product expense of 0.25 percent results in a total annual cost of around 0.45 percent and a T-REX Score of 87 percent, roughly double the T-REX Score of some of Old Bay Street's largest mutual funds.

The biggest challenge with fee-for-service advisors may be finding one! The great majority of advisors still operate under the Old Bay Street high product fee model or charge a fee based on a percentage of assets. Be prepared to do a bit of a search and, if you are outside a major city, to consult with a fee-for-service advisor by phone or through Skype or something similar. And confirm up front that the advisor is truly fee-for-service with no products to sell. Check www.larrybates.ca for links to fee-for-service advisor resources.

The aim of investing is to earn, and keep, an attractive rate of return to power your own personal Wealth Formula. There are two fundamental types of investments or 'asset classes': stocks and bonds. These two asset classes offer very different potential rates of return and degrees of risk. Understanding the characteristics of stocks and bonds, how to invest in them, and what to avoid will provide the basic investment knowledge and confidence you need to choose New Bay Street and select your preferred method of Simply Successful Investing—AIY, DIY, or robo. Stocks and bonds are the focus of the next two chapters.

7

Stocks

Stocks are dynamic investments
combining growth potential with volatility.

THIS CHAPTER EXPLAINS what you need to know about Simply Successful Investing in stocks. (Step by step guidance regarding actually selecting and buying stocks and stock index ETFs will be provided in Chapter 12.)

Simply put, a 'stock' is a fractional ownership share in a company. Stocks may also be called common stocks, shares, or equities. ('Preferred shares' are a completely different animal; see appendix.) Own a stock and you are a business owner. For example, if you own 100 shares of RBC, you actually own part of RBC, all its assets and profits. Sure, you own only a tiny bit of RBC, but you are an RBC owner nonetheless! And you have the same rights as any other owner, large or small.

With historical average annual returns of 7–10 percent, the North American stock market is one investment class in which compounding magic has truly worked wonders. The key to building wealth for most long-term Canadian investors will almost certainly be ownership of quality North American stocks (directly through purchases of stock in individual companies or indirectly through low-cost stock index ETFs).

The Stock Market

'Stock market' is a generic term referring to (i) an 'exchange' such as the Toronto Stock Exchange or the New York Stock Exchange, through which stocks are bought and sold or (ii) a major stock 'index' (or basket of stocks) such as the S&P 500 (500 largest US stocks) or S&P/TSX 60 (60 largest Canadian stocks).

Stock market news reports, such as 'the Dow fell by 120 points today' or 'Toronto stocks are now up 6 percent so far this year' are making reference to changes in the value of major stock indexes, which in turn reflect the sum total of changes in the prices of all stocks represented within these indexes.

What's Your Type?

Stocks can be grouped into various categories or sectors. These sectors can be based on geography (Canadian, US, UK, European, Asian, Global, Emerging Markets, etc.), industry (Financials, Utilities, Energy, Base Metals, Consumer Products, Retail, Technology, etc.), company size ('large cap' for big companies, 'small cap' for smaller ones), etc. Most major stock sectors are tracked by one or more stock indexes. Stocks are also broadly categorized by risk into 'blue chip,' speculative, and medium risk stocks.

Blue Chip Stocks

Blue chip stocks are shares of large, well-established, consistently profitable companies with a broad base of loyal clients and the proven ability to manage through economic downturns. Blue chip companies often pay out a portion of their profits in the form of con-sistent (and sometimes growing) quarterly dividends to stock holders. Think of Bell Canada, Canadian Pacific Railway, the big Canadian banks, Johnson & Johnson, Microsoft, and Coca-Cola to name just a few. Blue chip stocks form the core of the largest stock index ETFs, as well as most DIY investor portfolios.

Speculative Stocks

Often tempting and always risky, speculative stocks lack the sta-bility of blue chips. Some will produce fabulous gains while others will crash and burn. Trust me, you won't be able to tell the differ-ence until it is too late. And while they may appear 'cheap,' many spec stocks with exciting potential are priced to perfection; in other words, their stock price already reflects an expectation of spectacu-lar success and anything less will result in the stock tanking. Think penny stocks (stocks trading at prices below one dollar), technology companies in an early stage of development or reliant on a single product line, small mining or oil exploration companies, debt-laden retailers in a downward cycle, and the like. The list goes on and on.

Direct investing in speculative stocks is for insiders and expe-rienced professionals only. So, if you are an average investor, there is only one conclusion to draw: absolutely, 100 percent and forever, avoid direct investment in speculative stocks!

Moderate Risk Stocks

In terms of track record, consistency, and overall resiliency, medium risk stocks lie somewhere between blue chips and speculative stocks. Only consider direct investment in medium risk stocks under expe-rienced professional advice.

Stocks don't necessarily remain in their categories. Many blue chip companies like Apple and Microsoft started out as specula-tive. Meanwhile, some blue chip companies lose their touch and slip down to medium risk or speculative categories. And every now and then, a former blue chip star goes completely dark. Nortel Net-work's 2009 bankruptcy is a particularly prominent and painful Canadian example.

Stock and ETF Symbols

Stock exchanges assign short symbols to all stocks and ETFs. Any reference to a company, a company's stock, or an ETF in this book may include the symbol—or may just use the symbol only. For example, when referring to Bank of Montreal, we may use the stock symbol (BMO), and when referring to the iShares S&P/TSX 60 Index ETF, its symbol (XIU) may be used.

Capitalism for the Masses

The stock market is surely among humankind's greatest inventions. The most powerful wealth machine ever built, the stock market 'democratizes' capitalism in two distinct but related ways.

First, the stock market enables fast-growing businesses to raise needed cash by broadly selling shares to all types of investors. Think of Google, Apple, TD Bank, or Telus. Companies with shares publicly traded on stock exchanges (known as public companies) initially raised funds by selling shares to investors through an initial public offering (IPO). Many public companies will, from time to time, finance further growth by selling additional new shares to the public.

Second—and most important to you—*the stock market makes business ownership available to anyone with even modest means.* In the past, wealth creation through ownership of large businesses was the exclusive realm of the wealthy. Today, wealth creation through ownership of large businesses is open to anyone who has a few thousand dollars to invest.

The stock market enables you to purchase shares in companies at exactly the same market price as the largest institutional investors pay. As a shareholder of a public company, regardless of how you spend *your* day, thousands of your employees will spend *their* day on their primary mission: creating wealth for you. And you don't have to lift a finger. All the benefits of business ownership without any responsibility—now that is a beautiful thing! And when you are ready to sell your shares, you also get the same market price as the largest institutions.

The stock market can be used (and misused) in many ways, including as a casino for speculators and as raw material for creating crappy, expensive Old Bay Street investment products. Successful long-term investors use the stock market primarily as an efficient means of owning great businesses.

Business ownership, largely through publicly available stocks, is the world's primary wealth generator. Billionaires get rich by owning businesses. Pensions for government workers and union members, as well as your future Canada Pension Plan payments, are financed through owning businesses. Average investors build their retirement nest eggs by owning businesses.

One Single Bet

Simply Successful Investing is about giving you the opportunity to significantly increase your investment returns by learning investment basics, thinking long-term, and minimizing costs. In my view, thinking long-term means making one single bet. Is it a bet *on the stock market?* No. It is a bet *through the stock market.* Long-term business ownership through the stock market is a bet on the continued ingenuity, dynamism, growth, and prosperity of today's North American businesses and tomorrow's budding entrepreneurs. It is a bet on continued wealth creation and the astonishing power of compounding.

Ignore the relentless purveyors of pessimism and remember that *those who have made this bet in the past have never lost in the long run. Never!* Simply Successful Investing is about (i) being relentlessly optimistic regarding the long-term future and (ii) ignoring the short-term 'noise' of the markets.

As a long-term investor, you are not a stock market player. You are a business owner. And business owners don't waste their energy fretting about daily changes in the 'market value' of their businesses.

They get on with their lives and so should you. Imagine owning stocks and not caring, or at least caring very little, what the market does from day to day and from month to month. Think about the potential benefits this business ownership mindset creates: less anxiety, greater confidence, enhanced peace of mind, more freedom to live your life, and a very high probability of a more prosperous future!

Stock Prices

In the short run, the market is a voting machine, but in the long run it is a weighing machine. BENJAMIN GRAHAM, AUTHOR OF *THE INTELLIGENT INVESTOR*

In order to keep some of our illustrations simple, markets are shown moving up at a constant rate—of course, this is not reality! Markets move up and down, sometimes violently, every hour, every business day, every month, and every year. Placing your money in the stock market for short periods can be akin to gambling. But measured over decades, North American stock markets have always moved higher. The following table and chart clearly demonstrate how time transforms stock market gambling into Simply Successful Investing!

Table 7.1: S&P 500 Returns 1926–2015[1]

Time Frame	Positive	Negative
Daily	54%	46%
Quarterly	68%	32%
One Year	74%	26%
5 Years	86%	14%
10 Years	94%	6%
20 Years	100%	0%

Stocks have traded on the New York Stock Exchange on more than 20,000 business days over the nine-decade period from 1926 to 2015. The S&P 500 Index was higher on 54 percent of those days and lower on 46 percent of those days. Therefore, on any given day, S&P 500 investors had a 46 percent probability of incurring a loss. If you are a conservative, risk-averse investor, that sounds like a lousy bet, but stretch out the investment time frame and the "bet" looks less like... well... less like a bet!

In fact, the longer your investment time frame, the higher your probability of gain. Over those ninety years, gains were produced in 74 percent of the one-year time frames, 94 percent of the ten-year time frames, and 100 percent of the twenty-year time frames! There wasn't a single twenty-year S&P 500 investment time frame over that ninety-year period that produced a loss. Over the full ninety-year period, the compound annual growth rate of the S&P 500 Index (with dividends re-invested) was around 10 percent. This would have turned a $1,000 investment in 1926 into a tidy $5.4 million in 2015.[2]

Over the long-term, there is only one single factor that determines the price of a company's stock: profits (or, more precisely, current and expected future profits). A company's profit growth may be exponential, steady, or meagre, while other companies will experience profit declines or losses to the point of collapse. Eventually, a company's stock price will always respond accordingly. In the long run, whether up, down, or sideways, profits pull price.

A diversified collection of stocks in a fund will likely demonstrate smoother collective profit growth, with big winners offsetting poor performers. The value of a stock index fund will ultimately respond to changes in the profitability of its underlying stocks. In the long run, whether up, down, or sideways, collective stock profits pull stock fund prices.

In the shorter term, the range of factors that influence stock prices is virtually endless.

- political events (e.g., Brexit, Trump)
- industry conditions (e.g., oil glut)
- interest rate changes

- economist forecasts
- stock analyst forecasts
- company management changes
- emotions/sentiment
- trends

The great majority of these short-term factors have little influence on the ultimate long-term performance of quality companies, but they create a very bumpy stock market ride! Stock investing requires a certain mindset. As a stock investor, *suffering short- and medium-term volatility is the price you must pay for potential long-term gains.* Long-term investing in a well-diversified portfolio of North American stocks has always been a roller-coaster ride with one magical difference: the exit platform has always been at a higher level than the entry platform!

Look at investing in stocks another way: the shorter your investment time frame, the more your experience will be shaped by the noise of the 'market,' and the more you are a market 'player.' The longer your investment time frame, the less the daily or weekly activity and trends of the market matter. Over time, market influences largely fade into insignificance. The longer you hold quality investments, the more your experience and outcome become that of a long-term business owner. Long-term investors don't rely on the behaviour of the market and may even have a negative perception of the stock market itself. Rather, long-term investors simply believe in one thing: the ability of North American businesses to collectively do what they have always done: grow profits over time.

Stock Funds

Investment diversity reduces risk. In a well-diversified portfolio, stocks that may underperform the market should be offset by outperformers. But if you own only a handful of stocks or concentrate your holdings in only a couple of sectors, for example energy producers or financials, you may risk having too few outperformers to offset underperformers.

As discussed earlier, rather than purchasing a large number of individual stocks to achieve diversification, investors can easily buy funds that hold large groups of stocks. Conveniently providing investors with ownership of a diversified mix of companies through a single investment is the primary advantage of these stock funds.

Quality stock funds can include not only solid blue chip performers, but also some exposure to a broadly diversified mix of moderate risk and speculative stocks, which might otherwise, as individual direct investments, be inappropriate for average investors.

The two main categories of stock funds are Exchange Traded Funds (ETFs) and mutual funds.

ETFs

ETFs trade on stock exchanges, can be easily bought and sold with a few clicks at a cost less than $10 per transaction, and generally charge much lower ongoing fees than comparable mutual funds. Canada's largest providers of ETFs are Blackrock (a large US-based global asset manager) through its iShares brand, Bank of Montreal, and Vanguard (the world's second largest fund manager). You can find links to these and other ETF providers at www.larrybates.ca.

While substantial at $150 billion as of February 2018,[3] the Canadian ETF market is only about one-tenth the size of the Canadian mutual fund market. But, for the reasons clearly detailed in this book, Canadian use of ETFs is growing fast. Investors in this country are finally waking up to the impact of high mutual fund fees and are starting to do something about it! There are two main types of stock ETFs.

1. Index ETFs

Buy index funds. It may not seem like much action, but it's the smartest thing to do. CHARLES SCHWAB, AMERICAN FINANCIAL EXECUTIVE

Stock Index ETFs are designed to mimic the performance of a stock index. As such, an index ETF will hold the same stocks in the same proportions as the index it is intended to track, such as the S&P/TSX 60 or the S&P 500. No 'Brilliant Stock Pickers' (BSPs) required!

As they require no 'active' stock-picking, index funds are often referred to as 'passive.' But I find this label highly misleading. If you are invested in stocks, your investment journey will be dynamic, not passive!

Index ETFs are, by far, the simplest and lowest cost stock funds available, and, therefore, the most efficient means of obtaining ownership of a diversified collection of Canada's or America's top businesses. The largest ETFs tracking the broadest stock indexes come with annual fees ranging from approximately 0.05 percent to 0.25 percent, while smaller ETFs tracking less prominent indexes may charge fees ranging up to 0.5 percent or 0.6 percent per year. As the table below shows, many index ETFs produce very high T-REX Scores and very low TRUE FEES.

Table 7.2: Selected Low-Cost Stock Index ETFs

MERs as per sponsor websites, April 2018

Index ETF	MER	T-REX Score	TRUE FEE
Canadian Stock Index ETFs			
BMO S&P/TSX Capped Composite Index (ZCN)	0.06%	98%	2%
TD S&P/TSX 60 Index (TTP)	0.08%	98%	2%
iShares S&P/TSX 60 Index (XIU)	0.18%	95%	5%
Vanguard FTSE Canada Index (VCE)	0.06%	98%	2%
US Stock Index ETFs			
iShares Core S&P 500 Index (XUS)	0.10%	97%	3%
BMO S&P 500 Index (ZSP)	0.09%	98%	2%
Vanguard U.S. Total Market Index (VUN)	0.16%	95%	5%
Global Stock Index ETFs			
TD International Equity Index (TPE)	0.20%	94%	6%
iShares Core MSCI All Country World ex Canada (XAW)	0.22%	94%	6%
Vanguard FTSE Developed All Cap ex North America (VIU)	0.23%	93%	7%

2. Active ETFs

Think of an 'active' ETF as a mutual fund light. A more recent innovation in the ETF universe, active ETFs offer BSP stock-picking rather than simple index tracking. Utilizing a wide variety of so-called 'enhanced' investment styles, such as 'multi-factor,' 'tactical,' 'strategic,' 'momentum,' and 'alternative,' active ETFs come with varying layers of complexity designed to justify much higher fees than simple index ETFs charge. Guess which type of ETF is most heavily marketed!

Old Bay Street recognizes there is a slow but unstoppable shift in investor preference from mutual funds to ETFs. The recent proliferation of active ETFs represents Old Bay Street's attempt to direct as much of that shifting money into higher-fee ETF products. Active ETFs charge annual fees generally ranging from 0.50 percent to more than 1.00 percent, producing T-REX Scores in the 70s and 80s. I recommend Assemble-It-Yourself investors stick to lower-cost index ETFs and ignore the growing proliferation of cleverly marketed active ETFs.

Mutual Funds

As I am sure you now know, by far the most prolific and most profitable Old Bay Street product is the mutual fund. Let me be clear. As of February 2018, Canadians entrust $1.48 trillion of their precious savings to high-fee mutual funds[4] that are managed by shockingly ineffective BSPs and produce consistently miserable results.

The following quotes are from the 2016 SPIVA Canada Scorecard, the 'de facto scorekeepers' of Canadian stock mutual fund performance:

> "All observation periods and categories resulted in inferior fund performance relative to the benchmark."
> "Over the ten-year period, zero funds were able to outpace the S&P/TSX Canadian Dividend Aristocrats."
> "Over the longer term... the results are unequivocal... data show the losing pattern repeating across all categories."
> "Not a single manager investing in the US Equity fund category was able to deliver higher returns than the benchmark."

Scott Barlow of *The Globe and Mail* aptly described this failure as "a remarkable feat of probability-defying industry incompetence." But it actually isn't particularly surprising. Mountains of evidence have consistently shown that, in aggregate, mutual fund BSPs underperform the market to a degree roughly equivalent to the fees they charge.

If you want to maximize long-term returns and your ultimate retirement income, avoid high-cost mutual funds and practice Simply Successful Investing! If you already own high-cost mutual funds, get out! (See 'Trigger Warning' sidebar on page 58.)

Canada? USA? Global?

Which stock markets will give you the best shot at maximizing your investment returns? No one can forecast the best combination of Canadian and non-Canadian stocks, but it is virtually certain that in order to diversify risk and optimize returns, you need both.

O Canada!

There are lots of great Canadian public companies. If you are a DIY investor, your stock portfolio should include some of them, and approaches to selecting blue chip stocks will be addressed in Chapter 12. If you invest through a robo-advisor, a portion of your portfolio will automatically be invested in Canadian stocks. What about AIY investors?

AIY investors can choose from a number of low-cost index ETFs that contain baskets of Canadian stocks. A good example is the iShares S&P/TSX 60 Index ETF (XIU), which was launched in 1990, making it the world's first ETF. This ETF, which has an MER of 0.18 percent, holds a portfolio of stocks matching the composition of the S&P/TSX 60 Index, the most widely followed index for tracking large Canadian stocks. You can find a complete list of the stocks included in this ETF at www.blackrock.com/ca. But for now, here are the top twenty stocks in the iShares S&P/TSX Index ETF (as of April 6, 2018) as well as a chart displaying the breakdown of industries that make up the total holdings of the ETF:

Table 7.3: iShares S&P/TSX 60 Index ETF Top 20[5]

Company As of April 2018	Ticker Symbol	Weight	Sector
Royal Bank of Canada	RY	8.81%	Financials
Toronto Dominion Bank	TD	8.26%	Financials
Bank of Nova Scotia	BNS	5.78%	Financials
Suncor Energy Inc.	SU	4.70%	Energy
Canadian National Railway	CNR	4.39%	Industrials
Enbridge Inc.	ENB	4.23%	Energy
Bank of Montreal	BMO	3.89%	Financials
Canadian Imperial Bank of Commerce	CM	3.11%	Financials
BCE Inc.	BCE	3.08%	Telecommunications
Transcanada Corp.	TRP	2.93%	Energy
Manulife Financial Corp.	MFC	2.92%	Financials
Canadian Natural Resources Ltd.	CNQ	2.92%	Energy
Brookfield Asset Management Inc. Class A	BAM.A	2.70%	Financials
Nutrien Ltd.	NTR	2.35%	Materials
Canadian Pacific Railway Ltd.	CP	2.02%	Industrials
Sun Life Financial Inc.	SLF	1.98%	Financials
Telus Corp.	T	1.67%	Telecommunications
Alimentation Couche Tard Sub Voting	ATD.B	1.58%	Consumer Staples
Magna International Inc.	MG	1.52%	Consumer Discretionary
Waste Connections Inc.	WCN	1.45%	Industrials

The companies with the highest total market values have larger 'weightings' in this ETF. For example, 8.81 percent of the funds in this ETF are invested in RBC (Canada's most valuable company) while 1.45 percent is invested in the much smaller Waste Connections Inc.

Déjà Vu?

Have a quick look at the top stocks in the previous S&P/TSX 60 Index list. Do some of them look familiar? Recall the top 10 lists of the RBC Canadian Dividend Fund and the Renaissance Dividend Fund (sponsored by CIBC), shown earlier on page 90. Every single one of the stocks on those two BSP top 10 lists are drawn from the top 13 stocks on the S&P/TSX 60 Index list. These BSPs are simply picking Canada's largest stocks! And they are charging MERs of 1.76 percent (RBC) and 2.15 percent (Renaissance/CIBC), approximately ten to twelve times the MER charged by the iShares S&P/TSX 60 Index ETF, to do it. Just saying!

Figure 7.1: iShares S&P/TSX 60 Index – Industry Breakdown[5]

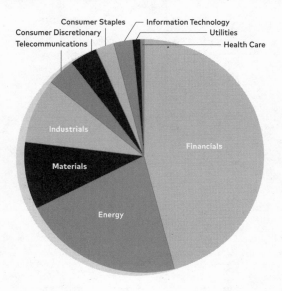

The mix of industries represented in this and many other Canadian stock index ETFs reflects the heavy concentration of Canada's stock market in financials and natural resource–related companies (energy and materials/mining). The Canadian stock market has only minimal representation in major, high potential sectors of the global economy, such as technology, health care, aerospace, consumer products, consumer finance, etc. And Canadian stocks represent less than 3 percent of the global stock market.

In order to achieve real diversification in your stock holdings, to own great businesses across a wider array of high potential industries, you must reach beyond our national borders.

Buy America

Our neighbour to the south possesses by far the largest, most diverse, most innovative, and most successful economy the world has ever known. Put America to work for you!

DIY investors looking to buy US blue chip stocks face a major challenge. There are so many hundreds of great companies to choose from. For AIY investors, even though the US market is so much larger, just like in Canada there are very simple and effective means to own US stocks in the form of low-cost index ETFs. And if you choose to go the robo-advisor route, a portion of your investments will automatically be allocated to ETFs that hold US stocks.

The most widely followed index for large American stocks is the S&P 500 Index, which includes 500 large American public companies and represents approximately 75 percent of the total value of all US stocks.

Canadians seeking to invest in the S&P 500 index can choose among a number of ETFs, like the Vanguard S&P 500 Index ETF (VFV) with an MER of 0.08 percent, which give you an ownership interest in each of the 500 companies represented in the index. Here are the top twenty S&P 500 stocks and their percentage weight in the Vanguard S&P 500 Index ETF as of February 2018 as well as a breakdown of the industries comprising the index:

Table 7.4: Vanguard S&P 500 Index ETF Top 20[6]

Company As of April 2018	Ticker Symbol	Weight	Sector
Apple Inc.	AAPL	3.92%	Technology Hardware, Storage & Peripherals
Microsoft Corp.	MSFT	3.10%	Systems Software
Amazon.com Inc.	AMZN	2.59%	Internet & Direct Marketing Retail
Facebook Inc. Class A	FB	1.82%	Internet Software & Services
JP Morgan Chase & Co.	JPM	1.71%	Diversified Banks
Berkshire Hathaway Inc. Class B	BRK.B	1.63%	Multi-Sector Holdings
Johnson & Johnson	JNJ	1.50%	Pharmaceuticals
Alphabet Inc. Class C	GOOG	1.43%	Internet Software & Services
Alphabet Inc. Class A	GOOGL	1.41%	Internet Software & Services
Exxon Mobil Corp.	XOM	1.38%	Integrated Oil & Gas
Bank of America Corp.	BAC	1.34%	Diversified Banks
Wells Fargo & Co.	WFC	1.11%	Diversified Banks
Intel Corp.	INTC	0.99%	Semiconductors
AT&T Inc.	T	0.96%	Integrated Telecommunication Services
Visa Inc. Class A.	V	0.96%	Data Processing & Outsourced Services
Cisco Systems Inc.	CSCO	0.95%	Communication Equipment
UnitedHealth Group Inc.	UNH	0.94%	Managed Health Care
Pfizer Inc.	PFE	0.93%	Pharmaceuticals
Home Depot Inc.	HD	0.91%	Home Improvement Retail
Chevron Corp.	CVX	0.91%	Integrated Oil & Gas

Figure 7.2: Vanguard S&P 500 Index ETF Industries[6]

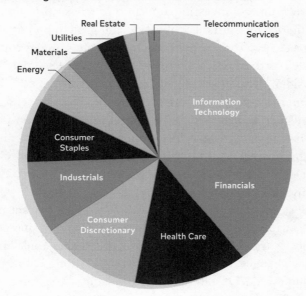

Note the significantly broader mix of industries represented in the S&P 500 Index compared to S&P/TSX 60 Index. And, at 25 percent of the index, the largest industry sector represented is technology. Buy an S&P 500 index ETF and you automatically own companies like Apple, Amazon, Alphabet (Google's parent company), and others, without undue overexposure to the individual technology risk of any one of them.

A final point worth noting: as most major US companies are multinationals with global business and global revenues, when you own the S&P 500 you own a good chunk of the global economy as well.

You can find a complete list of the stocks that make up the Vanguard S&P 500 Index ETF at www.vanguardcanada.ca.

Global Stocks

You may choose to place most, if not all, your non-Canadian stock investments in the US market. But, of course, there are stock markets in developed and developing countries around the globe. Many experts recommend investing a portion of stock portfolios outside North America for both diversification and growth potential.

As an AIY investor, if you choose to allocate some of your portfolio outside North America, there are a number of low-cost ETFs you may consider, including the Vanguard FTSE Developed All Cap ex North America Index ETF (VIU) with a 0.23 percent MER. Or you could consider an even simpler solution to owning non-Canadian stocks. Instead of separately buying both a US stock ETF and a non-North American stock ETF, you could buy a single non-Canadian stock ETF such as the iShares Core MCSI All Country World ex Canada Index ETF (XAW) with a 0.22 percent MER.

Business ownership creates wealth. The stock market provides average Canadians the opportunity to acquire great businesses at the same price as the biggest players. Business owners don't care about day-to-day changes in the market valuation of their businesses, and neither should you. Despite short-term volatility, long-term investing in a diversified mix of North American stocks will continue to be the cornerstone of Simply Successful Investing. You can bet on it!

8

Bonds

Bonds are static investments
currently offering low returns.

WHILE STOCKS ARE dynamic investments combining volatility with significant upside potential, bonds are static, or at least more stable, investments providing generally fixed rates of return with limited or no upside potential. With feeble fixed interest rates of around 2.5 percent or so, *today's bonds are virtually useless at building wealth.* Compounding loses almost all its magic at these low rates. Add in the impact of any fees, the punitive tax treatment of interest income (unless in a tax-sheltered account) and inflation, and the real purchasing-power gains of bonds may be near zero or, even worse, turn negative.

Are you inspired? I didn't think so.

So why would anyone want to own these anemic investments? Because bonds can be highly effective in *protecting* wealth. And wealth protection can be an indispensable component for investment portfolios, especially during the years leading up to and during retirement. And remember, even if bonds produce only 2.5 percent or so in annual interest over many years, that is far superior to your money earning zero, or close to it, while just sitting in a bank account!

In this chapter you'll find what you need to know about Simply Successful Investing in bonds.

A bond is a type of 'loan contract.' You are likely familiar with loan contracts if you have a mortgage, a student loan, or a car loan. Under these kinds of loan contracts, you are the *borrower* with these general terms:

1. A bank or other lender provides an upfront loan to you.
2. You promise to pay interest to the bank at an agreed rate and frequency.
3. You promise to repay the loan on an agreed date or series of dates.

Bonds and Guaranteed Investment Certificates (GICs) are simply loan contracts with the roles reversed. You are the lender. The borrower, or 'issuer,' of the bond or GIC is obliged to make interest and principal payments to you.

Each GIC is a discrete, tailored contract between you and a financial institution. In other words, you are the sole 'lender' under a GIC contract. On the other hand, each bond is a standardized contract between one borrower and hundreds or thousands of lenders, each of whom owns a fractional share of the same bond.

Most bonds and GICs pay a fixed rate of interest (sometimes called a 'coupon') with the full principal repayment amount due on the final maturity date. For example, the cash flows of a five-year $10,000 GIC with annual interest payments of 2 percent would look like this:

1. You pay $10,000 for the GIC.
2. On each anniversary of your purchase you receive a $200 interest payment.
3. On the fifth anniversary your $10,000 is repaid to you (in addition to the final $200 interest payment).

Some GICs are 'cashable,' meaning that they can generally be cashed out at any time without penalty, as the name implies. But most GICs are 'non-cashable' until the end of the agreed term. Some 'non-cashable' GICs may be cashed out early at a penalty. In any case, GICs cannot be sold or transferred to another party. Bonds work the other way around. Bonds cannot be cashed out early by the investor but can be sold at any time for cash at market value.

GICs are issued only by financial institutions, including banks, trust companies, credit unions, 'caisses populaires,' etc.; whereas bonds are issued by a wide range of borrowers including federal, provincial, and municipal governments, their agencies, large corporations, and the big banks.

The primary objective of all GIC and bond investors should be the safe return of the principal amount invested. Therefore, the financial strength of the borrower (or guarantor) is the essential consideration in selecting a bond or GIC. Bonds promising higher returns generally come with higher risk of non-payment.

The other main factor driving the differences in bond rates of return is term to maturity. Under most market conditions, the longer the term to maturity of a bond or GIC, the higher the rate of return. For example, as of April 2018, 2-year Government of Canada bonds were available at a yield of 1.8 percent while 10-year Canada bonds were on offer at a 2.15 percent yield. Investing in a longer-term bond or GIC may produce a better ultimate result if interest rates remain at current low levels; whereas, if rates rise, a series of shorter-term bonds or GICs may ultimately prove more rewarding. GICs are typically issued with maturities of one to five years while bonds usually come with original terms of three to thirty years.

Bond Prices

Upside down. Downside up.

Bond prices increase when interest rates fall. And bond prices decrease when interest rates rise. What the…?

The rationale for bond price changes can be difficult to grasp. It may be easy once you get it, but until then it can seem counter-intuitive. The next few paragraphs provide a brief explanation, but if it's too much of a mind bender, don't worry! You don't need to invest in individual bonds. Just buy bond index ETFs or GICs.

Okay, here we go. The market value of a bond will most likely differ from its face value. Prices of existing fixed rate bonds tend to rise with lower interest rates and/or increased financial strength of the borrower. Conversely, prices of existing fixed rate bonds tend to fall with higher interest rates and/or reduced financial strength of the borrower.

Let's say you buy a $10,000 bond that pays a coupon of 2 percent, or $200, annually for five years. The total payments you will receive over five years will be $11,000, which includes $1,000 in total interest as well as the $10,000 return of principal. What will happen to the market value of your bond as interest rates change?

Let's say interest rates drop and investors are willing to buy new five-year $10,000 bonds with an annual coupon of 1 percent from the same borrower. These bonds will produce $10,500 in total payments, including $500 in total interest as well as the $10,000 return of principal. If investors are willing to pay $10,000 for a five-year bond that will return $10,500, those same investors would naturally be willing to pay more than $10,000 for a five-year bond that will return $11,000. Therefore, your 2 percent bond is now worth more than $10,000.

Now let's assume interest rates increase and the same borrower must offer 3 percent coupons to attract investors. These bonds will produce $11,500 in total payments over five years, including $1,500 in total interest as well as the $10,000 return of principal. If investors now require a return of $11,500 for a $10,000 five-year bond, those same investors would not be willing to pay $10,000 for a five-year bond that will return $11,000. Therefore, your 2 percent bond is now worth less than $10,000.

For a given shift in interest rates or financial strength, changes in the market value of long-term bonds will be much greater than price changes of shorter-term bonds. For example, a 1-percent increase in interest rates would cause the market price of a three-year $10,000 bond to decline by around 3 percent or $300; whereas a $10,000 thirty-year bond would likely drop in price by around 20 percent or $2,000. (Note that bond market price changes don't much matter if you hold a bond to maturity.)

Safe and Sound

Shopping for GICs? Unless you are absolutely, 100-percent comfortable that the financial institution offering you GICs is completely bulletproof, make sure all your GICs are government insured.

The Government of Canada, through Canada Deposit Insurance Corporation (CDIC), insures most Canadian dollar denominated deposits, including most GICs with an original maturity of no more than five years, up to a maximum of $100,000 per insured category, per CDIC member financial institution.

Insured categories include regular accounts, TFSA accounts, and RRSP accounts. So, for example, if you have $75,000 in total deposits, including GICs, in a TFSA with a CDIC member bank or trust company, and another $75,000 in total deposits including GICs in an RRSP with the same bank or trust company, your total of $150,000 is covered. If you plan to have total GICs and any other deposits exceeding $100,000 within one insured category, you can split your business among CDIC member institutions so that all of your deposits are fully government insured.

For details on how CDIC insurance works and what is covered, and for a complete list of member institutions, go to www.cdic.ca.

All Canadian provinces operate deposit insurance programs for credit unions and caisses populaires. You can easily find the rules that apply in your province with an internet search.

Investing in Bonds and GICs

GICs can be obtained directly from the financial institutions that issue them, while both traditional Old Bay Street brokers and New Bay Street online discount brokers offer access to a wide selection of GICs, bonds, and bond index ETFs.

The world of bonds can be highly complex and the range of investment choices endless. But I have great news! Simply Successful

Investing can be achieved in the wealth protection component of your portfolio by choosing among three very straightforward types of bond investments:

1. Government-insured GICs issued by financial institutions offer a great combination of simplicity, return, and safety. But buy a regular, 'non-cashable' GIC only if you are reasonably certain you won't need access to your cash prior to the GIC maturity date.

2. Short-term Canadian bond index ETFs (such as Vanguard's Canadian Short Term Bond ETF [VSB] with a 0.11 percent MER, BMO's Short Provincial Bond Index ETF [ZPS] with an MER of 0.28 percent, and iShares Core Canadian Short Term Bond Index ETF [XSB] with a 0.10 percent MER) hold dozens or even hundreds of bonds and automatically reinvest in new bonds as old bonds mature. This provides bond index ETF investors the benefit of automatic diversification and the convenience of permanence. Unlike a bond or GIC, a bond ETF never matures. You can cash out any time by selling your ETF at the prevailing market price. (Market prices of short-term bond index ETFs fluctuate but not significantly so.) With fees averaging 0.10–0.30 percent, bond index ETFs produce T-REX Scores of 80–95 percent. It's that simple!

3. High-quality government bonds issued by the federal government and the provinces are an option if you have at least $25,000 or so to invest. (Note that bonds issued by Canadian provinces offer yields higher than federal government bonds.) If you choose to buy individual bonds directly, I recommend sticking with less volatile, shorter maturity bonds (five years and under) so you get the opportunity to acquire new, higher coupon bonds sooner if interest rates move up. If you are buying bonds in a regular, non-tax-sheltered account, stick to bonds priced close to, or less than, their face value. (There can be punitive tax consequences to buying premium-priced bonds in taxable accounts.) Like bond ETFs, government bonds can be sold anytime at market price.

Generally, GIC and bond investors do not pay fees directly. However, GIC issuers earn a 'spread' by lending out your money to someone else at a higher rate while brokers build a commission into the price at which bonds are offered.

Mutual Fund Madness

Stay away from Old Bay Street bond mutual funds! Like bond index ETFs, bond mutual funds provide diversification and permanence. Of course, the big problem with bond mutual funds is fees. Combine current low interest rates with high mutual fund fees and there is precious little return left for the hapless Canadian mutual fund investor.

As an example, let's look at the $2.8 billion CIBC Canadian Bond Fund; according to Morningstar Fund Finder,[1] the average bond yield to maturity in this fund is 2.02 percent while fees are 1.43 percent. Assuming yields and fees remain static, investors in this fund will receive an annual net return of only 0.59 percent (2.02 percent minus 1.43 percent). In this example, the one-year T-REX Score is 29 percent and the TRUE FEE is 71 percent. And the longer the projected time horizon, the worse it gets.

Add in the potential impact of the other two Wealth Killers—taxes and inflation—and many high-fee bond mutual funds actually *destroy* wealth. How can Old Bay Street keep promoting and selling high-fee bond mutual funds? It's madness.

If you want a bond fund, stick to low-cost index funds!

Off Balance

Canadians love 'balanced' mutual funds. Attractively packaged as a simple and convenient combination of both growth potential and protection, balanced mutual funds incorporate a mix of both stocks and bonds. A balanced mutual fund is essentially a stock fund and a bond fund stapled together. For example, the giant, $23 billion RBC Select Conservative Portfolio Fund, which sports a 1.84 percent MER, comprises approximately 40 percent stocks and 60 percent bonds.[2] Investing in a 40/60 balanced mutual fund is essentially the same as maintaining 40 percent of your funds in a stock mutual fund and 60 percent in a bond mutual fund.

High-fee balanced mutual funds are conveniently lucrative for Old Bay Street and simply awful for investors. Don't fall for this Old Bay Street packaging. If you choose robo-investing, an appropriate stock/bond mix will be automatically created for you. And as an Assemble-It-Yourself (AIY) or Do-It-Yourself (DIY) investor, you can create the right mix of stocks and bonds at a fraction of the cost of a balanced mutual fund. Just keep it simple and minimize costs.

The particulars of buying bonds, bond ETFs, and GICs are described in Chapter 12.

9

Mindset

Rip Van Winkle would be the ideal investor.
He'd invest before his nap, and when he woke up
twenty years later, he'd be happy.

RICHARD THALER, ECONOMIST AND
2017 NOBEL PRIZE WINNER

S IMPLY SUCCESSFUL INVESTING requires self-knowledge and self-discipline. Whether you are just starting out on your investing journey or shifting from Old Bay Street to New Bay Street, it is critical that you first develop the right investment 'mindset.'

Over the long-term, the stock market has consistently yielded positive returns. But we know that, from time to time, the stock market *will* decline significantly. Not *could* decline significantly. *Will* decline significantly—and frequently! This is an absolute certainty. But no one knows exactly when or by how much. You must accept this reality, treat stock market downturns as perfectly normal, and not react to them. With Simply Successful Investing, you are in it for the long haul. Learning to drown out the noise of the markets will enable you to achieve a far better investing outcome.

The Enemy Within

The greatest enemies of the equity investor are expenses and emotions.
JACK BOGLE, FOUNDER OF THE VANGUARD GROUP

The old investment chestnut 'buy low, sell high' may sound easy. But realistically, in the heat of the moment, our emotions scream out the exact opposite. Sadly, the lure of quick gains and/or the fear of missing out compels legions of investors to buy when the noise is positive and the prices are high. And overwhelming fear compels many poor souls to sell when they just can't take it anymore, when prices are at their lowest and all hope seems lost.

Let's go back to 2007; stock markets were hitting all-time highs and Canadian stock market investors were feeling mighty fine about the fabulous gains they had experienced over the previous few years. In the meantime, many savers who had avoided the risk of the stock market could no longer handle missing out on the action and jumped in. But by the fall of 2008, stock markets around the world were in full panic mode as the global financial system seemed on the verge of collapse, with diminished economic activity and mounting job loss.

Many Canadian investors experienced 30–40 percent declines in the value of their stock portfolios, and many 'experts' predicted (hourly and breathlessly) the worst was yet to come. Unable to withstand the stress and unwilling to risk further 'paper' losses, thousands of investors crystallized those losses by dumping all their stocks and mutual funds. A very unfortunate reaction, but totally understandable. The fear was palpable and pervasive, but selling 'locked-in' these severe but short-term market losses. Investors sold their 'businesses,' most of which continued to be very profitable, at fire sale prices, and were left watching from the sidelines as the economy recovered, companies once again began to produce record profits, and stock prices reached record highs. Many retirement dreams were permanently lost.

The Emotional Cost

Studies show that Canadian investors actually lose billions through buying high and selling low. Morningstar's May 2017 "Mind the Gap" research report shows the typical Canadian stock mutual fund investor's return over the past ten years was reduced by an annual average of 1.38 percent due to buying high and selling low.

How does this typical behaviour impact ultimate investment results? In our thirty-five-year-old Ables illustration, it is assumed that their investment pattern was constant. But what if the Ables behaved like the average Canadian and earned 1.38 percent less on their stock funds? The Ables' annual investment income in retirement would be reduced by about one quarter, from $45,800 to $33,900.

Meanwhile, forever frozen by mistrust of Old Bay Street sales pitches or fear of stock market volatility, millions of potential long-term investors remain on the sidelines, simply leaving their savings in the bank earning little or no interest. A 2015 survey[1] conducted by BlackRock showed that only 19 percent of Canadians' financial assets are invested in stocks. By choosing not to participate in the stock markets, millions of Canadians are forfeiting the potentially lucrative rewards of long-term business ownership and, in the long run, will suffer as a result.

Misconceptions about the markets can make you into your own worst enemy when it comes to investing. Achieving the benefits of Simply Successful Investing requires that you not only learn investment basics, but also learn to tune out the noise—in the markets, in the media, and in your own head. To keep your emotions from getting in the way of your investing success, you must:

1. Recognize fear and greed
2. Accept fear and greed
3. Ignore fear and greed

Adopting the Simply Successful Investing approach—and sticking to it no matter what the markets are doing—will enable you to stay the course and earn healthy long-term returns.

Balancing Act

Investment philosophy is really about temperament, not raw intellect. In fact, proper temperament will beat high IQ all day. MICHAEL MAUBOUSSIN, COLUMBIA BUSINESS SCHOOL

What portion of your portfolio should be dynamically invested in stocks versus listlessly invested in bonds? Determining your stock/bond balance may be your most important investment decision.

Invest in stocks only to the extent you are *committed*—as a business owner—to ride out market storms, because the storms will come. As a worst-case scenario, let's assume that at some point there will be up to a 50 percent decline in stock markets during a future economic crisis, similar to the darkest hours of the 2008–09 global financial crisis.

Ask yourself this question: What level of short-term losses in my total overall portfolio am I prepared to *tolerate* during a stock market crash? Your 'tolerable loss' ratio can provide a useful rule of thumb when it comes to determining the right mix of stocks and bonds for your portfolio.

If your 'tolerable loss' is zero—in other words, if you aren't prepared to suffer any losses whatsoever, even short-term losses—you are in full wealth-protection mode. You should own zero stocks.

What if you are willing to accept the risk of short-term losses up to around 25 percent of your total portfolio in order to have the high probability of long-term gain? In our worst-case scenario of a 50 percent market crash, the total value of a $100,000 portfolio split 50/50 between stocks and GICs would decline by 25 percent to $75,000. (The stock portion would decline in value from $50,000 to $25,000 while the GIC value remains constant at $50,000.) Like the Meeks when they started out, if your tolerable loss is 25 percent you should place no more than 50 percent of your investable assets in stocks with at least 50 percent placed in GICs or bonds.

If, however, you are like the Ables when they started out, and are committed to weather the storm of a potential short-term 50 percent market meltdown in order to capture 100 percent of the ultimate long-term growth of the stock market, you may choose to be 100 percent invested in stocks.

Mentally preparing yourself, as a business owner, for regular stock market declines of 10–20 percent, occasional declines of 30 percent or more, and even extreme scenarios like the 2008–09 crash and determining your stock/bond allocation accordingly is fundamental to the kind of long-term thinking necessary for Simply Successful Investing.

Risky Business?

American author Denis Waitley said, "There is only one big risk you should avoid at all costs, and that is the risk of doing nothing."

We naturally think of risk as something to be avoided.

For example, Dictionary.com defines risk as "exposure to the chance of injury or loss; a hazard or dangerous chance: as in, 'It's not worth the risk.'"

But the truth is, our daily lives are loaded with all sorts of risk; every choice we make, from playing a sport to commuting to work to choosing a life partner to selecting a restaurant menu item, involves risk. Consciously or not, we assess the potential risks and rewards of the decisions we make and either proceed, adjust, or step away accordingly. We take some risks and avoid others. In other words, we manage risk. It is the same in the realm of investing.

Trader or Investor?

The stock market is a device for transferring money from the impatient to the patient. WARREN BUFFETT

True stock market investing—business ownership—is a steady, long game: a *marathon.* You won't find much discussion or advice on BNN or CNBC or other media about long-term investing. At any particular moment in time, it simply isn't particularly exciting to discuss. And there is not much to debate. It just works!

Trading or 'playing' the stock market by attempting to profit from frequent, sometimes daily, buying and selling of stocks is a volatile, short-term game: a *sprint.* Trading is a completely different game with different rules, different goals, and different players. You will find endless discussion and advice about stock trading on BNN or CNBC and many other broadcast, print, and online media. And there is constant debate—but it just doesn't work!

Table 9.1: Investor vs Trader

	Investor	Trader
Daily Focus	Life	The Market
Long-Term Performance	Paramount	Irrelevant
Short-Term Performance	Irrelevant	Paramount
Time Frame	Years or Decades	Minutes or Months
Investment Timing	Market Agnostic	Market Driven
Inspirational Animal	Tortoise	Hare
Olympic Event	Marathon	Sprint

Can you name any Olympic 100-metre-sprint gold medalists? I can name a few: Donovan Bailey, Ben Johnson (only for a few hours!), and the aptly named Usain Bolt. Sprinters are easy to remember because the event is flashy and lightning fast.

Can you name any Olympic marathon gold medalists? Not many people can! Do the names Eliud Kipchoge and Jemima Sumgong sound familiar? Both are incredibly successful athletes, but we don't remember these 2016 Olympic champions because marathons are long and can be boring to watch. Dear friends, this is your event! Simply Successful Investing *is* a marathon. No one will know your name and your personal victory will be achieved quietly. Your friends and neighbours may not notice for years to come. Who cares? Accept it, relax, and enjoy the ride!

You won't feel compelled to brag about your brilliant trades over cocktails, which is good because that kind of talk is really boring and obnoxious anyway. And, more importantly, you won't suffer silently, feeling like crap about all your disasters.

Forget about the sprint. And when you hear the sprinters talking their game—and they always talk a big game—smile and pretend you care or, even better, move over to the cheese table. When you hear the analysts, economists, forecasters, and other 'sprint coaches' talk about their favourite stock or sector or country of the day, change the channel. Because it means absolutely nothing to you or your long-term investment success. Paying *zero* attention to short-term stock market movements can be both liberating and lucrative. Don't be a day trader, be a decade trader!

Leave Well Enough Alone!

The following excerpt from a Columbia Business School press release sums up nicely what long-term Simply Successful Investing is all about:

"Michaela Pagel, assistant professor of finance and economics at Columbia Business School, and an expert in 'household financial decision making,' shows that when people do check their holdings frequently, and attempt to rebalance on their own, they make investment decisions they believe will decrease pain and increase happiness—but which often leave them worse off financially over time.

Her suggestion? Simply check your portfolio less often."

Invest Like Clockwork

As you build your portfolio, commit to a regular investment schedule. Whether you choose to place your money in the stock market quarterly, semi-annually, or annually, stick to your schedule regardless of how the market is performing. I call this 'Clockwork Investing.' It's easier said than done when the market is trending down and all the 'noise' is negative, but in the long run it will work for you.

Table 9.2: Investing Patterns

	Disciplined Marathoner	Undisciplined Marathoner (closet sprinter)	Sprinter
Strong Market	Buy	Buy	Buy
Neutral Market	Buy	Buy	Uncertain
Weak Market	Buy	Sell	Sell
Result	Matches Market Performance	Severe Underperformance	Severe Underperformance

'Disciplined marathoners' invest like clockwork. They invest steadily whether the market is moving up, down, or sideways. And when withdrawing cash from the market during retirement, they remain indifferent to market moves and use exactly the same 'steady as it goes' approach. Those who attempt the investment marathon by buying steadily during rising and stable markets, but who lose their nerve during falling stock markets and either stop buying, or worse still, begin selling, will fall far behind. Meanwhile, the vast majority of sprinters will crash and burn on a steady diet of buying high and selling low.

But what if, as a result of coming into a chunk of cash from an inheritance, home downsizing, sale of a business, a retirement package, or some other windfall, you have a large amount to invest in stocks? You may risk buying high at the top of the market. As an alternative to making single, large stock market actions, consider immediately investing only a portion of the amount you have earmarked for stocks, say one-quarter or one-third of the total, and commit to a shorter-term Clockwork Investing program for the balance, placing equal portions in the stock market at pre-determined dates over the next several months or couple of years. This technique, known as 'dollar cost averaging,' makes for a smoother ride when placing large amounts in the stock market. And spreading out major stock sales over a period of time provides the same type of smoothing effect when withdrawing funds as income or when reducing exposure to the stock market (for example, when shifting your asset mix more toward bonds).

10

Your Financial Plan

Q: What is the most frustrating
answer to any question?

A: It depends.

'**B**EGIN WITH THE *end in mind*.' According to the late author
Stephen Covey, this is the first of the seven habits of highly successful people. It is also fundamental to Simply Successful
Investing. You must have a sense of where you are going in order to
get there. But when it comes to planning for the long-term, including
for retirement, it is important to understand that there are no 'right'
answers. As with life in general, precision simply doesn't apply. Your
goals will change over time depending on your changing circumstances, life events, and priorities. Important planning variables like
investment returns, inflation levels, and your individual lifespan will
also have a major impact on your ultimate results and are impossible
to predict accurately. Consistently heading in the right general direction by regularly building savings and Simply Successful Investing is
much more important than the accuracy of any particular forecast or
the degree of detail of your plan.

Don't buy into the misleading notion promoted by Old Bay Street that their plans create wealth: you, your hard-earned savings, and smart long-term investing create wealth! That said, there is great benefit in having a plan, even a very simple one. Having a target, even though it will be a moving target, gives you a direction to shoot for and specific steps to follow.

In the next chapter, I will illustrate a few very simple financial plans covering a range of circumstances, but first let's focus on the biggest challenges associated with retirement planning by addressing three key questions.

Three Key Questions

What will my annual retirement costs be?

The answer depends on your lifestyle choices: where you choose to live, your desire to travel, your hobbies—as well as numerous things you can't control, like energy level, health, unexpected events, inflation, and so on. Experts suggest your retirement income should be between 50 percent to 100 percent of your working income. Everyone's circumstances are different, but that's a pretty wide range! You can assume your needs (and wants) will require an income somewhere between these two extremes. Assuming a ratio of 70 percent retirement income versus working income is a good place to start for most of us.

For those approaching retirement, *The Globe and Mail* provides a handy online 'Retirement Readiness Calculator.'[1] This tool includes a pre- and post-retirement expense checklist, which can help you estimate your retirement income needs. Just go online and search 'globe retirement readiness calculator' and try it out for yourself.

What size of retirement nest egg will I need?

The answer hinges on a multitude of factors, including your assured sources of regular income like Canada Pension Plan (CPP), Old Age Security (OAS), employer pensions, annuities, any significant sources of cash such as an inheritance or home downsizing, etc.

The 'Rule of 20' (developed by the Canadian office of Russell Investments) is a simplified method that gives you a very rough and rather conservative estimate of the size of nest egg you might require.[2] First, estimate the amount by which your annual retirement costs will exceed your assured sources of income (your 'Retirement Gap'). According to the Rule of 20, multiplying your Retirement Gap by twenty gives you a rough approximation of your required nest egg. For example, if your Retirement Gap is $25,000, your required nest egg according to the Rule of 20 would be around $500,000 ($25,000 x 20). But again, this is a generalization; everyone's circumstances are different and will likely change from time to time.

How much should I save?

By now, I am sure you know what's coming. The annual savings required to accumulate your retirement nest egg depends on when you start, how much you start with, your target retirement age, your stock/bond split, actual investment returns, and the variable impact of the three Wealth Killers: fees, taxes, and inflation. Again, given that there are so many uncertain factors, there is no right answer as to what percentage of your income you should save, but you can easily come up with rough estimates of target savings levels that match your circumstances.

Most major Canadian investment providers, including the big banks, offer online retirement calculators that produce estimates of the monthly savings rate required to achieve various retirement nest eggs and incomes. You can find links to a number of useful retirement calculators at www.larrybates.ca.

Some of the calculators produce results with minimal input. For example, in less than a minute, the TD Retirement Calculator[3] will estimate a monthly savings rate with only your age, income, and the amount you saved to date as inputs. You can then make adjustments to your projected retirement age (initially set at age sixty-five) and retirement income rate (initially set at 70 percent of working income) to see how your monthly savings requirement varies. Other key assumptions such as investment returns, inflation rate, CPP, and OAS payments and longevity (age ninety) are hard-wired.

Other calculators require varying degrees of inputs and flexibility. Generally speaking, the more detailed the inputs, the more tailored and the more meaningful the results. Make sure to be reasonable when assuming investment returns and observe how sensitive your outcome is to different return assumptions. Remember: rate of return inputs are meant to be net returns after fees. For example, if you wish to try a scenario assuming total investment returns of 6 percent and you pay annual fees of 0.5 percent, input a return of 5.5 percent.

As you move through your fifties and into your sixties, you would likely benefit from a more fulsome retirement savings and income analysis. I suggest you spend some time with the federal government's Canadian Retirement Income Calculator.[4] This excellent tool, which is built to accommodate planning for individuals as well as couples, allows you to test out various retirement time frames and target incomes, assumed rates of return on investments and ages at which you plan to start receiving CPP and OAS payments, and incorporates various sources of income including RRSPs, employer pensions, TFSAs, annuities, etc. The calculator adjusts for inflation and produces a detailed report projecting income sources for each year of retirement, along with the resulting annual shortfalls or surpluses relative to your target income. You can easily adjust key assumptions, including RRSP and TFSA contribution rates, to assess the impact on your projected results.

Once you've considered your three key retirement questions, and perhaps have experimented with various planning tools to establish your goals for savings and retirement income, how do you turn those objectives into action? That's where a financial plan comes in; to translate your long-term financial goals into concrete action today and to keep you headed in the right direction.

Your Plan Options

Again, a financial plan is not a one-size-fits-all proposition. There are several ways to go about it, depending on your needs and your personality.

If at any time you feel uncomfortable with where you stand or where you are headed, either spend some additional time educating yourself or get some professional advice. Just recognize what you will pay for it.

The Un-Plan

If you are in your twenties or thirties and can't imagine retirement, let alone estimate your required nest egg decades in the future, just keep things simple! If possible, try to save at least 10–15 percent of your net income and put it toward (i) permanently paying down debt, (ii) investing (ideally within a TFSA or RRSP), or (iii) buying a home. And forget about retirement, at least for a few years. Review your progress annually and adjust accordingly. That's it!

The Self-Plan

If you are reading this book, and you have actually gotten this far, you are likely more than capable of self-planning your retirement finances. Utilize some of the retirement planning resources found at www.larrybates.ca and get comfortable using one of the more detailed retirement calculators discussed previously. Based on the required savings level suggested by the calculator, as well as the practical realities of your personal circumstances, determine an annual savings amount, commit to it, and apply your savings to permanent debt reduction or investment (in TFSAs and/or RRSPs to the extent possible).

By far the most important step in creating an effective financial plan is the easiest: write it down! If you choose to self-plan, do yourself a big favour: put your plan in writing and save it. We are all more likely to follow through on a plan if it is clear, documented, and we monitor our progress against it. So make it simple and keep track of your progress annually.

The Fee-for-Service Plan

If you are comfortable with Simply Successful Investing but feel you need some professional financial planning help, fee-for-service advice may be appropriate for you. You might want guidance from an advisor consistently throughout your investment journey, or on occasion to supplement your un-plan or self-plan. As discussed earlier, fee-for-service planners offer truly independent professional advice because their compensation is not dependent on the sale of financial products like investments and insurance.

Fee-for-service planners use retirement calculators and other software to help provide advice about target nest eggs and required savings rates, but also cover areas such as optimizing the use of RRSPs, TFSAs, and RESPs; family budgeting; insurance and estate planning; and other planning services for those with more complex financial affairs. As previously discussed, you can find fee-for-service advisors online or through referrals. Take advantage of the free initial consultation that is generally offered and, if you are comfortable proceeding with a particular advisor, there should be an agreement in advance (by way of an engagement letter) on the range of advice, scope of the plan, number of meetings, time frame, follow-up, and cost.

The Old Bay Street Plan

As discussed earlier in this book, if you want Old Bay Street 'advice' you can easily get some—for free! It will cost you only your time. Remember, without a clear, honest discussion regarding the impact of costs, Old Bay Street 'advice' is really just a sales pitch. That said, recommendations regarding a savings plan, use of RRSPs and TFSAs, and your stock/bond asset mix (and any other guidance other than recommendations to purchase expensive products) may actually be objective and helpful.

Do some window shopping. Drop into your bank branch. Reach out to your insurance provider. Talk to a broker. Confirm you can get some advice without committing to invest. Make it clear that cost will be an important consideration for you in any final decisions, and you may find a sincerely friendly, helpful advisor. But be on the lookout for those Old Bay Street tactics like fear, bewilderment, complexity, false salvation, etc.

Take your Old Bay Street plan home. Give it some thought. If you see some merit in the plan, make whatever adjustments you think are appropriate, then decide whether to execute the investment element of your plan through expensive Old Bay Street products, or through New Bay Street at a fraction of the cost. If you really believe Old Bay Street products are best for you, make absolutely certain you understand all fees and use the T-REX Calculator to see the impact of those fees before you commit. Otherwise, just step over to New Bay Street and execute your plan through an online discount broker or robo-advisor. If you choose to go with an online discount broker, some Old Bay Street advisors may actually direct you to that division within their firm (if they have one).

What Is Fair? #3

Knowing that you likely won't end up buying their expensive products, would you be comfortable obtaining free 'advice' from your bank or another Old Bay Street provider?

Recognize that offering absolutely free, no-obligation plans is just part of Old Bay Street's Pitch, Plan, Product, Prize strategy to sell you overpriced products. For Old Bay Street and their advisors, you and your money are fair game. In my view, it follows that accepting an offer of a free plan should be an altogether fair part of your relationship with Old Bay Street.

And even if you ultimately choose low-cost New Bay Street products, you likely have paid, or will eventually pay, thousands of dollars in investment, banking, mortgage, credit card, and other costs and charges to Old Bay Street over your lifetime.

Whichever planning approach you choose, keep it simple, commit to your plan, and stick to it as best you can. Save and invest like clockwork regardless of market conditions. But also make sure to adjust your financial plan from time to time to reflect your changing needs, and the twists and turns in your life that you simply can't predict. For example, determine your target stock/bond mix at the outset and make appropriate adjustments as your financial and over-all life circumstances change. It's a good idea to review your situation and update your plan annually—or at least bi-annually. This exercise doesn't have to take a lot of time; the important thing is to keep your plan simple, relevant, and meaningful.

Save Yourself!

I made my money the old-fashioned way. I was very nice to a wealthy relative right before he died. MALCOLM FORBES, PUBLISHER OF *FORBES MAGAZINE*

If, like Malcolm Forbes, you are fortunate enough to have accumu-lated, inherited, or will otherwise come into sufficient resources to meet all your future financial needs, then congratulations! You don't need to save. What about the rest of us?

Spending less than you earn and saving the difference must be the foun-dation of every financial plan.

Although we can never have a perfectly accurate vision of our future financial needs, most of us acknowledge the need to save because government and employer pensions will fall well short of our retirement needs. And while the ability (and requirement) to save usually ends at the point of retirement, the need to keep spending in check is a lifelong endeavour.

Talking about saving is easy. *Actually* saving is hard. It's a tough balancing act that requires discipline: giving up current, very tan-gible benefits for uncertain benefits in the distant future. It means trading the pleasures of spending and consumption today for the abil-ity to live better tomorrow. In other words, saving requires 'delayed gratification.' Let's be honest, self-imposed delayed gratification can be very tough to achieve and maintain. Especially when we are pum-melled every day by an endless array of temptations to spend.

There are numerous sources of advice on how to save: online, in books and newspapers, and through other media. Most offer useful insights and solid, common-sense guidance. You can find links to useful advice on saving at www.larrybates.ca. But the following is a quick overview of saving basics.

Before saving for the future, you need to do two things. First, eliminate all high-cost debt, including credit cards. With interest charges of 15 to 25 percent, credit cards are like Wealth Killers on steroids. Get your credit card balance down to zero and keep it there by fully paying it off every month. If you have extra costs and can't completely pay down your card in a given month, direct every bit of available cash to pay it off as soon as you can.

Second, build up an emergency fund and tuck it away in a savings account. Many experts recommend maintaining an emergency fund equivalent to three months of living costs.

These first two steps may take some time, but once your high-cost debt is paid off and you have built up an emergency fund, you are in a position to begin building long-term savings. This may require some up-front planning. Over a period of several weeks, I suggest you keep track of every single penny spent by you and your spouse— if you have one. There are two ways to look at this: as a pain in the butt, or as a voyage of discovery. Your choice. But for many, this has the potential to be a real eye opener. You may be very surprised at how much you spend on certain items. Give some careful thought to the results. Separate your spending into 'needs' and 'wants' and start thinking about the trade-offs you may wish to make in order to increase monthly savings.

With a better understanding of your spending, you can more easily create a realistic budget. There are dozens of online budgeting tools, calculators, and spreadsheets. You can find links to particularly useful sites at www.larrybates.ca. Once you have created your budget (which hopefully calls for spending less than you earn!) do your best to stick to it. Perfection is not required, but a degree of discipline certainly is. Your budget may include short-term saving for major expenses like an annual vacation or an automobile purchase, as well as long-term wealth building. The portion of your savings aimed at building wealth must either be invested for the long-term or go toward permanent debt reduction. (Permanent debt reduction means accelerated reduction of debt like student loans and mortgages, while maintaining your rate of monthly payments so that the principal balance of your debt is reduced at a quicker pace. Paying down a line of credit only to re-borrow later doesn't count!)

Many experts recommend directing at least 10 percent of your income to long-term savings. But both the ability to save and the need to save for retirement are different for each of us. Of course, as demonstrated in Table 3.1 on page 33, the earlier you start, the better the end result. The later you start saving, the more you need to save. Whether you create a plan on your own or get savings advice, you must be the final judge of what is right for you.

Be Great, Automate

Do yourself a huge favour and arrange to have your regular savings automatically transferred from your main bank account to a separate savings account each payday. From this savings account, funds can be periodically (quarterly, semi-annually, or annually) transferred to your TFSA, RRSP, or regular investment account and invested according to your Clockwork Investing plan. Even better, skip a step by transferring funds directly from your bank account to your investment account each payday—if the service is available.

Automating the savings process doesn't prevent you from temporarily holding back transfers to your investment account when you need to. That's okay, perfection is not necessary. But automation builds savings with one single action rather than being dependant on you taking action on every transfer date.

One final observation on saving: there are many chronically stressed middle-class Canadians, and even top-earning Canadians, who live large but never get ahead. And there are many more content, happy Canadians who live more modestly while they slowly but surely become millionaires, or close to it. Be one of these happy Canadians! Also, hang out with these happy Canadians. Why? Because happy people are more fun, and it will be a lot easier to keep up with the 'modest' Joneses than the 'living large' Joneses!

11

Sample Plans and Portfolios

Tomorrow belongs to the people
who prepare for it today.

AFRICAN PROVERB

W E ALL HAVE unique hopes and dreams—and a different capacity to save—and 'real life' plays out differently for each of us. As a result, both our ability to save, and our investment objectives, will evolve over time.

Reading through each of these sample plans will give you some ideas about how you can apply the principles of Simply Successful Investing to your own financial plan. These plans are not meant to encapsulate every circumstance—far from it—but one of them may roughly fit your situation. More likely parts of a few of these scenarios may have some useful application for you today or in the future.

Homeward Bound

At age twenty-nine, Jenny's goal is to build up enough savings to make a sizeable down payment on her first home by age thirty-five. She has $30,000 sitting in the bank and believes she can save another $6,000 annually. Jenny has a good understanding of investing basics, and she is comfortable taking an Assemble-It-Yourself approach to investing. She opens a TFSA account through an online discount broker and transfers her $30,000 savings into the new account.

Given her relatively short-term, six-year investment horizon, Jenny decides to direct two-thirds of her funds to GICs and one-third to a Canadian high-dividend, blue chip stock ETF. She takes the following steps:

1. Buy a $20,000 CDIC-insured two-year GIC paying annual interest at a rate of 2 percent.
2. Invest $10,000 less $10 commission in a Canadian blue chip stock ETF with a dividend yield of 4 percent and an MER of 0.25 percent and enrol in the automatic distribution reinvestment plan (also known as a DRIP).
3. Annually transfer $6,000 in additional savings to the TFSA account.
4. Annually apply $4,000 of the new funds, plus interest earned on GICs as well as proceeds from any maturing GICs, toward the purchase of new GICs.
5. Annually invest $2,000 less $10 commission in the same Canadian blue chip stock ETF.
6. Sell the ETF at a commission cost of $10 at age thirty-five.

Assuming Jenny's GICs continue to pay 2 percent interest over the six-year investment period, her total GIC investment of $40,000 (the original $20,000 plus $4,000 annually for five years), as well as the re-investment of interest received, generates proceeds of $43,756 at age thirty-five. The gain of $3,756 is simply the total interest earned on the GICs over the six years.

The proceeds of Jenny's total ETF investment of $20,000 (the original $10,000 plus $2,000 annually for five years) will obviously depend on changes in the value of her ETF. If the price of her ETF units remains constant over her six-year investment time frame, Jenny's proceeds from the sale of her ETF will produce $23,576. The gain of $3,576 arises from the 4 percent reinvested dividends less the 0.25 percent MER and annual $10 commission costs. When combined with the $43,756 in proceeds from GICs, this would result in total cash of $67,332 available for Jenny's down payment. A 5 percent annual gain in the value of the ETF would boost Jenny's total portfolio value to $73,158 while a 5 percent annual loss in ETF value would bring her portfolio value down to $62,593. The following graph shows the proceeds of both the GIC and ETF investments based on the annual change in value of the ETF.

Figure 11.1: Jenny's Portfolio Value at Age 35

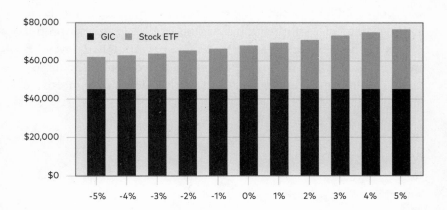

Jenny is willing to accept the risk that her ETF may perform poorly because the majority of her portfolio is guaranteed, and she believes the odds of favourable Canadian blue chip stock performance over a six-year time frame are stacked in her favour.

Jenny's Plan

Date:_____

Over the next six years, I will build a down payment to purchase a home. I will invest my savings of $30,000: two-thirds in GICs and one-third in a blue chip Canadian stock index ETF and reinvest all income earned. Over the next five years I will save $6,000 annually and invest on the same basis.

Less Is More

Tanya and Raj: Part One

Tanya and Raj are both thirty-five years old and first-time home owners with a substantial mortgage. Their medium-term 'investment' plan could not be simpler: cut their $500,000 mortgage in half.

'Investing' in a mortgage by making eligible principal prepayments can be as beneficial as, or even more powerful than, investing in bonds or stocks. The benefit of mortgage prepayment is simple: reduced future interest charges and getting rid of your mortgage sooner.

The terms of Tanya and Raj's mortgage are as follows:

Amount: $500,000
Rate: 4 percent
Amortization: 25 years
Monthly Payment: $2,630
Prepayment Option: Up to 10 percent of the original principal amount annually without penalty

Assuming mortgage renewals at the same 4 percent rate, it would take seventeen years to get their mortgage balance down to

$250,000 if they simply made their regular monthly payments. But Tanya and Raj apply their total annual savings of $15,000 to pre-paying their mortgage. When their mortgage renews, Tanya and Raj maintain their monthly payments at $2,630 and they continue to make $15,000 prepayments annually. At this pace, it takes only eight years to get their mortgage down to the $250,000 level they targeted.

Tanya and Raj's Plan (Part One)

*Date:*_____

We will cut our $500,000 mortgage in half over the next eight years by directing $15,000 in annual savings to eligible mortgage prepayments while maintaining our $2,630 monthly payments.

How much should you 'invest' in your mortgage? Investing 100 percent of your savings in paying down a mortgage can be a winning strategy, especially for those who do not want any stock market risk. Applying all long-term savings to mortgage paydown means giving up the potential that stock market returns will exceed your mortgage 'investment' returns (your mortgage rate) over time. Given that mortgage rates are so low, it won't take much for the stock market to outperform. So, some combination of mortgage prepayment and tax-sheltered stock investments (in TFSAs and/or RRSPs) probably makes sense for most Canadians.

Can a Penny Saved Beat a Penny Earned?

A dollar of mortgage interest saved is as good as a dollar of gains earned within a TFSA. But note that a dollar of mortgage interest saved is worth more than a dollar of interest earned outside a TFSA. This is because gains outside TFSAs will be taxed either immediately (if earned in a regular non-sheltered account) or eventually (if earned in an RRSP). I am sure the government would love to find a way to tax mortgage interest savings, but thankfully they haven't figured that one out yet!

Couch Potatoes

Tanya and Raj: Part Two

At age forty-three, Tanya and Raj feel pretty good about accomplishing their goal. They managed to cut their $500,000 mortgage in half! They are comfortable with their remaining $250,000 mortgage balance knowing that, by continuing to maintain their $2,630 monthly payment rate, their mortgage will be completely paid off within ten years without the need for any further prepayments. Tanya and Raj have built up substantial room to contribute to TFSAs and RRSPs but have not yet done so.

With a goal of having the ability to comfortably retire twenty years later, at age sixty-three, Tanya and Raj begin investing their annual $15,000 savings through TFSAs. Once their mortgage is paid off at age fifty-two, Tanya and Raj decide to start contributing to RRSPs as well. Given their 40 percent marginal tax rates, they know that their tax bills will be reduced by 40 percent of their RRSP contributions, so they decide to make total RRSP contributions of $52,600 annually. After tax refunds totalling $21,040 (40 percent of $52,600), their net out-of-pocket annual cost of RRSP contributions will be $31,560 which exactly matches the annual total of the monthly mortgage payments (twelve payments of $2,630) they are no longer making.

When they begin investing at age forty-three, Tanya and Raj are comfortable placing all of their investments in stocks, but plan to reduce their stock allocation over time as detailed below.

To execute their plan, Tanya and Raj select a low-maintenance, 'couch potato' portfolio of low-cost index ETFs (MER of 0.25 percent) purchased through an online discount broker. Assuming long-term pre-fee stock index ETF returns of 7 percent and bond index ETF returns of 2.5 percent, this AIY approach would generate an annual retirement income of $34,000 from their TFSAs and $45,000 from their RRSPs for a total of $79,000 from age sixty-three through age ninety.

Tanya and Raj's Plan (Part Two)

*Date:*_____

We aim to build a nest egg sufficient to enable both of us to comfortably retire at age sixty-three, should we choose to do so. We will direct $15,000 in annual savings to TFSAs. Beginning at age fifty-two when our mortgage is fully paid off and our monthly payments cease, we will make contributions to RRSPs such that we remain cash neutral. We will invest our TFSA and RRSP savings in low-cost stock and bond index ETFs, initially with a 100 percent stock allocation, subsequently shifting to 75 percent at age fifty-three, 50 percent at age sixty-three, and finally to 25 percent at age seventy-three.

Automatic for the People

Michael has just paid off his student loans and has tucked away an emergency fund of a few thousand dollars. He is ready to start investing his monthly savings and has a good understanding of investing basics, but Michael prefers a super-convenient, fully packaged solution. He does a bit of shopping around online and finds a robo-advisor he is comfortable with.

Michael answers the online questions, follows the prompts, is satisfied with the recommended mix of ETFs, signs up, and arranges $500 monthly transfers from his bank savings account to his robo-advisor TFSA account. From time to time over the years, as Michael's circumstances or investment objectives shift, he has discussions with a *real human* at his robo-advisor, and suitable changes are made to his savings plan and portfolio mix.

Assuming Michael sticks with his $500 monthly contributions and earns an average annual investment return of 6.5 percent after fees, Michael's nest egg after thirty years will be worth over half a million dollars. This will be music to Michael's ears. (To those of you who don't know the band R.E.M., apologies for the inside joke!)

Michael's Plan

*Date:*_____

I aim to steadily build my savings over the next few years. I will automatically transfer $500 monthly to my robo-advisor TFSA account. I will revisit my plan and update it if required in two years.

The Canadian Classic

Like millions of Canadians, Jason and Chris want to both pay down their mortgage *and* save for retirement. And they find an elegant solution: they are each able to save $5,000 annually, and in January of each year they contribute their prior year's savings to their respective RRSP accounts and invest according to their desired stock/bond splits. Their RRSP contributions reduce their taxable income, and each gets a tax refund after filing their returns. If their net taxes owing before taking their RRSP into account are zero, and both have a 45 percent marginal tax rate, both Jason and Chris would receive $2,250 in annual refunds from CRA. Applying these tax refunds to eligible mortgage prepayments reduces their mortgage principal balance by $4,500 each year. Jason and Chris achieve both their goals, benefitting significantly from both the tax-free compounding within their RRSPs and the rapid paydown of their mortgage.

Jason and Chris's Plan

*Date:*_____

We will steadily build our RRSP investment portfolios and reduce our mortgage by annually contributing a total of $10,000 to RRSPs and applying the resulting combined $4,500 tax refunds to eligible mortgage prepayments.

The Great Escape

By their mid-fifties, Charles and Marie have built up good-sized RRSPs. But they are worried; their Old Bay Street brokerage statements show several mutual funds, a few blue chip stocks, and a rotating collection of stocks they have never heard of. They long ago gave up the struggle to understand their complex portfolios and get no meaningful planning advice. Like my sister Mary, they eventually discover they have lost a shockingly large portion of their investment returns to high mutual fund fees. And losses among their 'no-name' stocks have negated strong returns earned on their blue chips.

Ultimately, Charles and Marie realize something has to change. They don't relish leaving their advisor but refuse to continue paying the price of sticking with the status quo.

Charles and Marie open new RRSP and TFSA accounts at their bank's online discount broker and arrange for their existing portfolios to be transferred. They keep their blue chip stocks but decide to replace their mutual funds and no-name stocks with low-cost index ETFs.

Given they can see retirement on the horizon, Charles and Marie decide to 'invest' some of their fee savings in a retirement plan from a fee-for-service advisor.

With a simple, low-cost portfolio that they actually understand, and a professional plan tailored to their objectives, Charles and Marie get on with their lives, worry a lot less, get better investment returns, and keep more of those returns for themselves.

Charles and Marie's Plan

*Date:*_____

We will greatly simplify our investment portfolio, reduce cost, and obtain a financial plan that will act as our road map as we approach and enter retirement by (i) moving our investments to new accounts at our bank's discount broker, (ii) replacing mutual funds and speculative stocks with stock index ETFs, and (iii) consulting a fee-for-service professional financial planner.

12

Investment Selection

---

*Success is where preparation
and opportunity meet.*

BOBBY UNSER, PROFESSIONAL
RACE DRIVER

THIS CHAPTER COVERS the final step to Simply Successful Investing: the process of selecting your investments and buying index ETFs, stocks, and bonds.

Given the endless barking from Old Bay Street sprint coaches and their media cheerleaders about the overwhelming complexity and constantly changing dynamics of investing, how can this chapter be so short? Because Simply Successful Investing is, well, so simple! This chapter will give you the information and the confidence you need to turn the principles of Simply Successful Investing into action.

Once you have a plan (even if it's an un-plan) and begin to accumulate savings, or if you have decided to switch from Old Bay Street to New Bay Street, it's time to choose your new investment provider and set up your RRSP, TFSA, and/or regular accounts.

If you choose the robo-advisor method of Simply Successful Investing, you will be advised regarding your investment selection, and ETFs will automatically be purchased for you as you contribute funds to your TFSA, RRSP, or other accounts. If your fund transfers to your robo-advisor are automated, the annual maintenance required by you is literally zero.

While a great deal of support is available if you choose the AIY or DIY methods of Simply Successful Investing through an online discount broker, you must ultimately make your own investment choices. This is the case even if you work with a fee-for-service advisor, because while they may offer guidance regarding stock/bond mix and the merits of certain types of investments, such as ETFs versus mutual funds, they are likely not licensed to recommend specific investment products.

The Big Switch

If you have Old Bay Street TFSA, RRSP, or other accounts and you are ready to switch to Simply Successful Investing, you need to transfer the assets from those old accounts to matching accounts at your New Bay Street investment provider. As long as you switch from one tax-sheltered account to another of the same type (as in RRSP to RRSP, and TFSA to TFSA) there will be no tax consequences. You just carry on. If you switch out of a regular, non-sheltered account and sell assets (like mutual funds) to reinvest in new assets (like index ETFs) there may be tax consequences (see 'Trigger Warning,' page 58).

Once your New Bay Street accounts are set up, you will be provided with the required transfer forms. Just complete the forms and your New Bay Street provider will send them to your Old Bay Street firm, which will process the transfer. This process usually takes two or three weeks, and your Old Bay Street friends may stick it to you one last time by charging annoying account transfer fees.

AIY Stock Investing

Once you determine your stock/bond mix and your preferred geographic allocation, you can assemble your stock index ETF portfolio. You could just keep it simple at 50 percent Canadian stocks and 50 percent American stocks; if you want to include global stocks, you may wish to go with 40 percent Canada, 40 percent US, and 20 percent non-North American, or even one-third each.

For the Canadian portion of your AIY stock portfolio you can simply choose a single ETF, such as Vanguard's FTSE Canada Index ETF (VCE) with a 0.06 percent MER; or iShares S&P/TSX 60 Index ETF (XIU) with an MER of 0.18 percent, both of which hold 60 or so of Canada's top companies; or an index ETF that focuses on blue chip dividend-paying Canadian stocks such as Vanguard's FTSE Canadian High Dividend Yield Index ETF (VDY) with an MER of 0.22 percent.

The easiest way to own America's top companies is through an ETF that tracks the world's most widely followed stock index: the S&P 500. There are several to choose from, including BMO S&P 500 Index ETF (ZSP) with an MER of 0.09 percent, iShares Core S&P 500 Index ETF (XUS) with an MER of 0.10 percent, and Vanguard S&P 500 Index ETF (VFV) at an MER of 0.08 percent. (I own a few US stocks directly but the majority of funds I have invested in US stocks are in index ETFs.)

Some index ETFs are tailored to Canadians looking to own non-North American stocks, including BMO MSCI EAFE Index ETF (ZEA) with a 0.22 percent MER, and Vanguard FTSE Developed All Cap ex North America Index ETF (VIU) with a 0.23 percent MER.

Another approach to owning non-Canadian stocks would be to purchase a single 'ex Canada' index ETF that includes American and global stocks, such as iShares Core MSCI All Country World ex Canada Index ETF (XAW) with an MER of 0.22 percent and Vanguard FTSE Global All Cap ex Canada Index ETF (VXC) with an MER of 0.27 percent. Just over half of the value of both of these ETFs is in US stocks, with the balance largely spread around Europe and Asia.

The simplicity of this AIY stock investing approach is depicted in the following three illustrative portfolios:

Figure 12.1: AIY Stock Portfolios

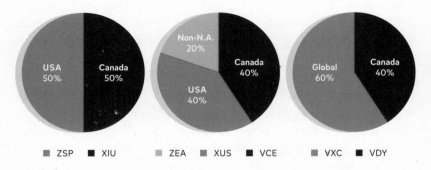

AIY stock investing can really be that easy. Just like the Ables, you can invest in, and stick to, just two or three stock index ETFs over your whole investment lifetime.

If AIY stock investing makes sense to you, you may not want to deal with the added complexity of DIY investing. But, keep in mind that true DIY investors achieve T-REX Scores of up to 99 percent, so I suggest you take a few minutes to read about how you might successfully employ a DIY investing approach. Over time you may wish to own a few blue chip stocks directly to complement a largely AIY approach.

DIY Stock Investing

Buy and hold a stock for the long-term, and you become a direct owner of a business and the profits it produces now and over time. Why is this Simply Successful Investing method Bay Street's worst nightmare? Because buying a stock directly through a discount brokerage account can cost you less than $10 in fees, with the same modest cost when you ultimately sell. You will pay no fund management fees or MERs to anyone. Aside from the cost of the trades, every penny of the returns you earn is yours to keep.

For example, if you invest $10,000 in a stock that generates a 6 percent average annual compound return over thirty years within your TFSA or RRSP, your total gain would be $47,435. In this case the final score would read as follows (assuming $7 commissions at the time of purchase and sale):

Gain You Keep: $47,421
Portion of Gain Lost to Bay Street: $14
Your T-REX Score: 99.99 percent

Nightmare on Bay Street!

DIY stock investing requires building a diversified portfolio of many stocks. This can be daunting for some, but a very rewarding approach for those with a strong understanding of investment basics. There are tens of thousands of successful DIY investors across Canada; I am one of them. Rather than own Canadian index ETFs, I directly own a collection of blue chip Canadian stocks, almost all of which are among Canada's top 60 stocks. Given my experience in the business and the way I built my portfolio over time, it makes sense for me to invest directly in Canadian stocks rather than pay ETF fees. Many other experienced investors take the same view.

If you prefer a DIY approach to owning Canadian stocks, start with the bluest of blue chips. Build a portfolio from Canada's top 20 stocks and make sure you diversify across industries to the extent possible as you build. Venture beyond the top 20 only after you have gained significant experience and knowledge.

Clone the BSPs. Ditch the Fancy Fees!

Despite all the evidence to the contrary, do you still believe in the stock-picking skills of Old Bay Street's Brilliant Stock Pickers? As revealed in the Old Bay Street Secrets chapter, all Canadian mutual funds are required to list their top stock picks, so you can build a portfolio matching the top ten list(s) of your favourite BSP(s). If you choose to mimic the moves of your favourite BSPs over time, you can do so by monitoring changes in their publicly available top 10 lists. But don't necessarily expect much activity. Most leading BSPs change their top picks very infrequently.

What about US and global stocks? DIY investors can take the same portfolio-building approach as with Canadian stocks. The wonderful thing is that there are so many hundreds of great companies to choose from but, as mentioned earlier, this also presents a major challenge! Most DIY investors in US or global stocks can attain only a fraction of the tremendous diversity available through index ETFs. In my view, in order to benefit fully from that diversity, even the most experienced DIY investors should allocate a sizable portion of their US and/or global stock portfolio to low-cost index ETFs.

Be the Banker!

One last note on DIY stock investing: I haven't pulled many punches when it comes to the way Old Bay Street banks treat average Canadian investors. But I don't want to leave you with the impression that I don't like the banks. The truth is, I love Canadian banks! And you can learn to love them, too.

What's the most beneficial possible relationship you can have with a Canadian bank?

1. Account holder
2. Credit card holder
3. Mortgage borrower
4. Online banking customer
5. None of the above

The correct answer is 5, none of the above.

The most rewarding relationship you can have with a bank is to be an owner. At least that has been the case throughout all living memory.

Major Canadian banks have been, and continue to be, remarkably powerful money-making machines producing strong growth in profits, dividends, and stock prices over the past sixty or seventy years. Risks are always present. Bank stock prices briefly lost half their value in the midst of the 2008–09 global financial crisis before recovering and ultimately reaching new all-time highs, and today there are concerns regarding an over-heated housing market and the risk of disruption from new technologies. No one can accurately predict the future, but there are good reasons to expect Canadian banks will continue to prosper in the long-term. Here are a few:

- the 'Big Six' banks have a dominant domestic market share
- competition from foreign banks is severely restricted
- the federal government provides substantial support to Canadian banks
- the banks are conservatively managed
- the long-term Canadian economic outlook is positive
- despite mixed feelings, Canadians implicitly trust their banks
- over the past century the major Canadian banks have a perfect record of paying consistent and growing dividends

If you think Bay Street banks overcharge, earn enormous profits, are protected by the government, generally get away with murder, and will continue to do so, there is a perfect way for you to address this 'inequity.' Include bank stocks in your portfolio. Make bank profits work for you.

Love your bank. If you want to *beat the bank*, be the banker!

Buying Stocks and ETFs

People of a certain vintage may remember the first time they used an instant teller (ATM) or transferred funds online. Those simple actions that we now perform without a second thought once seemed quite disconnected from reality—or even scary. Investing your money online for the first time can feel equally strange and intimidating but doing so will be very empowering! Once again, I suggest you try the practice accounts offered by the online broker you are considering so you can become comfortable with the buying and selling processes before embarking on the real thing.

Place your orders to buy or sell stocks and ETFs during regular open hours of the exchange on which they trade. Both Toronto Stock Exchange and major US exchanges (such as New York Stock Exchange) are typically open from 9:30am to 4:00pm Eastern Time. All ETFs mentioned in this book, including US and global stock ETFs, trade on the Toronto Stock Exchange.

Each online discount broker is slightly different, but all guide you through a similar transaction execution process. Here is a summary of the steps you will typically go through to buy stocks and index ETFs through an online discount broker:

1. Select which of your accounts will be making the purchase (e.g., your TFSA account).
2. Select 'buy' as the type of order.
3. Enter the 'symbol' for the stock or ETF (e.g., XIU for iShares S&P/ TSX 60 Index ETF, or BNS for Bank of Nova Scotia common stock and so forth). Double-check to make sure the symbol exactly matches the stock or ETF you wish to buy. If you aren't absolutely sure, phone or chat with your online discount broker and ask!
4. Select Canada as the 'market' if the stock or ETF trades on a Canadian exchange.
5. Request a 'quote' to find the current market price of the stock or ETF.
6. Based on the amount of cash you wish to invest, determine the number of shares or units you want to buy. For example, if you want to invest approximately $4,000 in VDY, which has a current market price of, say, $32.55, you could theoretically buy 122 units. But if you have only $4,000 in cash, order slightly fewer, say 120

units, to allow for the commission cost of a few dollars and the possibility that the actual buy price may be slightly higher by the time your purchase is actually processed (stock and ETF prices literally change minute by minute). For example, if the final buy price is $32.57 per unit and you pay a commission of $9.99, your total cost would be $3,918.39 ($32.57 x 120 plus $9.99).

7. Select 'market price'—unless the market is temporarily in turmoil or the security you aim to purchase is obscure, in which case select 'limit price,' which allows you to set an upper limit on your purchase price.

8. Select 'good through day,' which means that your instructions apply for the current day only.

9. Select 'any part,' which means your order can be executed in parts (e.g., if your buy order is for 120 units, you may first receive a 'partial fill' of 100 units followed moments later by a second transaction for the remaining 20 units).

10. Select 'continue' to review a summary of your order including estimated total cost.

11. Carefully review your order.

12. Confirm your order.

13. You will receive order execution confirmations by email (there may be several emails if your trade is completed in parts).

Practice a few times before making your first actual purchase. If you are uncertain about any detail regarding buying a stock or ETF, get on the phone to your provider! Once you become familiar with the process, online buying of stocks and/or ETFs can take less than a couple of minutes to complete. And, depending on how often and how much you regularly transfer into your investment accounts, you need only make new purchases once or twice a year. Selling ETFs and stocks is just as easy and just as inexpensive.

Do yourself a favour. When you buy a stock or ETF, don't check the market price later in the day. It doesn't matter! What difference will the price in any given minute that day make five years or five decades from now when you sell? Virtually zero! Okay, okay, you can't help yourself, right? I get it. But here is the point: don't think for a second that you are smart if the market price of a stock or ETF goes higher in the hours or days after you buy it. And don't think you are a loser if the price falls. Remember, short-term market moves are meaningless—ignore them. You are engaged in Simply Successful Investing for the long-term.

Bond Investing

As discussed earlier, Simply Successful Investing in bonds can be achieved three different ways: through bond index ETFs, government-insured GICs, or high-quality government bonds. Just like stock ETFs, bond index ETFs trade on major exchanges, including Toronto Stock Exchange, and the steps involved in buying and selling bond index ETFs are identical to those outlined above for stock index ETFs. Given today's extremely low interest rates, I believe ETFs that hold shorter-term bonds are the best choice for most investors. Short-term bond index ETFs will benefit from rising rates sooner than other bond ETFs. There are several short-term bond index ETFs you can choose from, including:

- iShares Core Canadian Short-Term Bond Index ETF (XSB) with an MER of 0.10 percent
- Vanguard Canadian Short-Term Bond Index ETF (VSB) with an MER of 0.11 percent
- BMO Short Provincial Bond Index ETF (ZPS) with an MER of 0.28 percent

The following graphs illustrate the use of these bond index ETFs, as well as the stock index ETFs shown in the examples depicted in Figure 12.1 on page 168, to create portfolios with a stock/bond split of 80/20:

Figure 12.2: AIY Stock and Bond Portfolios

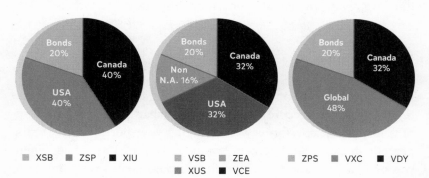

These sample portfolios are not oversimplifications. As an AIY investor, copying this exact approach, sticking to just three or four index ETFs, and adjusting your stock/bond mix over the years will give you everything you need for a lifetime of Simply Successful Investing. Choose this approach and you will reap the rewards of T-REX Scores in the 90s and rates of return likely double that of mutual funds, without ever having to pick a stock or bond, or risk betting on an Old Bay Street BSP.

If preferred, you can use GICs or direct bond purchases instead of bond index ETFs along with either AIY or DIY stock investing.

If you wish to buy GICs, follow your online discount broker prompts and select the payment frequency and maturity. You will then be presented with a list of issuers and GIC rates matching your request. You will find that the big banks usually pay rates below those offered by the smaller players. As discussed in Chapter 8, make sure your GICs are insured by CDIC or a provincial government agency.

Directly buying individual bonds through your online discount broker is also straightforward. You will be prompted to specify your requirements, including the type of issuer (Canada, provinces, municipalities, corporates), credit rating, preferred maturity range, and the approximate amount you wish to invest. (As discussed earlier, I recommend you stick with Canadian federal and provincial government bonds.) You will then be presented with a list of available bonds from which you can select. You will have the opportunity to review the details prior to confirming your purchase.

Rebalancing

Let's say you decide on a mix of 60 percent stocks and 40 percent bonds and invest accordingly. Fine. But what if the stock portion of your portfolio performs well, bringing your portfolio mix to 65 percent stocks and 35 percent bonds over time? First of all, when you own stocks, good stock performance is good news! But your exposure to stocks is now higher than you planned. Restoring your original 60/40 asset mix requires rebalancing your portfolio.

You should regularly re-evaluate your portfolio mix. Unless you experience a significant change in circumstances, an annual check-up is fine. If your mix hasn't changed by more than a few percent, you could let it ride for another year or simply direct any fresh portfolio contributions to the lower performing asset class (bonds in the case above) until the original balance is restored. If your asset mix has shifted more than a few percent, you could simply sell a portion of the over-performing asset class and direct proceeds to the underperforming asset class to restore balance.

In addition to rebalancing asset classes, you must be similarly mindful of maintaining balance across geographies and, if you are a DIY investor, among individual stock holdings.

Game Changer!

As mentioned in Chapter 8, Canadians love the simplicity and convenience of balanced mutual funds, which provide automatic ongoing rebalancing to maintain a target stock/bond asset mix. But high fees severely diminish the balanced mutual fund returns Canadian investors actually get to keep.

In February 2018, Vanguard launched Canada's first low-cost, glob-ally diversified, balanced ETFs. These 'Asset Allocation' ETFs offer the same simplicity, convenience, and automatic rebalancing offered by bal-anced mutual funds, but at a fraction of the cost. With an MER expected to be in the area of 0.25 percent, these balanced ETFs will produce T-REX Scores in the 90s while typical balanced mutual fund MERs of 1.5-2.0 percent will generate T-REX Scores in the 40s and 50s. Vanguard is offering a choice of three different stock/bond combinations:

Table 12.1: Vanguard Asset Allocation ETFs

ETF	Stock Allocation	Bond Allocation
Vanguard Conservative ETF Portfolio (VCNS)	40%	60%
Vanguard Balanced ETF Portfolio (VBAL)	60%	40%
Vanguard Growth ETF Portfolio (VGRO)	80%	20%

If one of these ETFs matches up with your desired stock/bond mix, you could continually invest in one single ETF until you decide to change your allocations. For example, if you want an 80/20 stock/bond split, you could direct all your TFSA or RRSP contributions to VGRO. Globally diversified, automatically rebalanced investing couldn't get much sim-pler! When you are ready to shift to a more cautious asset mix you could switch some or all of your portfolio to VBAL or VCNS.

The low cost balanced index ETF is a product whose time has come! I expect other providers will launch similarly attractive balanced index ETFs in the near future.

Fuel the Magic

As mentioned earlier, many companies—including most blue chips—pay out a portion of their quarterly profits to stockholders in the form of dividends. Reinvesting those dividends by buying more stock of the same company will maximize compounding and accelerate growth in the long-term value of your investments. Fortunately, most blue chips provide DIY investors the ability to choose *automatic* reinvestment of dividends in new company stock at the current market price, without paying any additional brokerage commission. This convenient feature, generally known as a Dividend Reinvestment Plan (DRIP), is there for the taking.

Most major ETF providers offer AIY investors a similar commission-free option to automatically reinvest distributions on both their stock and bond ETFs. Make sure to select these reinvestment options for as long as you are building your portfolio. Unlike most things in life these little pieces of compounding magic are free!

When it comes to GICs and direct bond holdings, simply reinvest interest payments whenever you have accumulated sufficient cash in your account and reinvest as soon as possible when your GICs or bonds mature.

Choose Your Path

Which method of Simply Successful Investing is right for you? Each New Bay Street approach has its pros and cons, but they all can produce results vastly superior to those found on Old Bay Street.

Robo-advisors can be the ideal solution for Canadian investors who seek the ultimate in hands-off convenience and are satisfied with T-REX Scores in the 70s and 80s.

AIY investing can be the optimal approach for Canadians who learn investment basics, want instant diversification and T-REX Scores in the 90s, and can spend a couple of hours a year making changes and additions to their portfolios.

DIY investing can be the best option for more experienced investors who can build diversified portfolios on their own to achieve T-REX Scores approaching 100 percent.

Some investors may shift or mix methods over time; after gaining more knowledge and confidence, some investors who start out with robo-advisors may later shift to AIY investing in order to reduce costs. And some AIY investors may partially incorporate the DIY method by directly buying a few blue chip stocks for their portfolio.

Choose the Simply Successful Investing method that you believe suits you best today. And if you need additional advice, consider getting it from an impartial, fee-for-service advisor.

13

Final Thoughts

Whatever you do, or dream you can,
begin it. Boldness has genius and
power and magic in it.

JOHANN WOLFGANG VON GOETHE,
GERMAN STATESMAN

SIMPLY SUCCESSFUL INVESTING through New Bay Street offers you the potential to double your long-term investment returns compared to traditional Old Bay Street products. Doubling your investment returns can give you the freedom to turn your dreams into reality.

In other words, Simply Successful Investing matters. And you can do it!

Make sure you have a good general understanding of how to power your own Wealth Formula. Maximize Wealth Builders to capture the magic of compounding and minimize the impact of Wealth Killers. Use the T-REX Score calculator to determine whether you will end up keeping a fair share of your returns.

Be aware of the powerful grip Old Bay Street has on you. Realize that Old Bay Street's Pitch, Plan, Product, Prize strategy is a sales pitch, not objective advice. Be an informed consumer and be wary of the dark side. Recognize that Old Bay Street does not create wealth— Old Bay Street extracts wealth. Wealth is created by you investing your hard-earned savings in long-term business ownership using low-cost products.

As a Simply Successful Investor, you are not a stock market player, you are a business owner. You aren't betting on the stock market. You are betting on the long-term growth of North American business through the stock market. Given time, this bet has always paid off.

Accept that, over the long-term, not investing is not an option. Ensure your asset mix reflects your risk tolerance. Expect stocks to decline at any time. Utilize bonds as the wealth protection portion of your portfolio, especially in the years leading up to and during retirement.

If you need help, get it. Just recognize that you will be paying for it, now and over time.

Nothing to Fear but Fear Itself?

If fear is preventing you from switching to New Bay Street, you're not alone. You may require further de-programming!

I suggest moving a small portion of your investments, or directing your next few fund transfers, to a New Bay Street provider. Just try it out. If it doesn't feel right, switch back to your current Old Bay Street provider. But I think you will find Simply Successful Investing through New Bay Street both liberating and highly rewarding!

Reject complexity. Embrace simplicity. Whether AIY, DIY, or robo, choose the method of Simply Successful Investing that best suits you.

Whichever path you choose, the right person will be in control of your destiny: you.

The Ten Commandments of Simply Successful Investing

As a final summary of this approach and a rallying cry to *beat the bank* by taking your financial future into your own hands, here are the top ten rules to keep in mind as you embark on your quest to double your investment returns through Simply Successful Investing:

1. Learn investment basics
2. Understand The Wealth Formula
3. Know your T-REX Score
4. Recognize how Bay Street operates
5. Be a long-term business owner
6. Know your risk tolerance
7. Make a simple plan
8. Invest like clockwork
9. Ignore the market
10. Enjoy life!

I hope Simply Successful Investing makes a difference in your life!

To learn more about Simply Successful Investing and to join a community of other Canadians seeking to invest smarter, please check out my website, www.larrybates.ca, subscribe to my newsletter, and follow me on social media.

Appendix

---

1. Tax-Sheltered Accounts

We have already discussed the use of TFSAs and RRSPs for tax-sheltered long-term investing. The following is a brief summary of the key attributes of three other types of tax-sheltered accounts as well as a brief discussion regarding the use of RRSPs for building first-time homebuyer down payments. You can get more information on these subjects online or through your investment provider.

Registered Education
Savings Plans (RESPs)

RESPs are tax-efficient accounts designed for saving for post-secondary education expenses for your kids, grandkids, or any other 'beneficiary' you may choose. Like TFSAs (but unlike RRSPs), contributions are not tax deductible and ultimate withdrawals of contributions are not subject to tax. Investment income and government RESP grants (yes, grants!) are not subject to tax until withdrawal and, if withdrawn by the student, will likely be taxed at a very low rate or not at all. To learn more, go to your browser and search 'resp comparison.' Warning: there is a whole set of Old Bay Street specialists selling extremely high-fee RESP accounts to unsuspecting new parents and grandparents. Set up your RESP accounts on New Bay Street!

Registered Retirement Income Funds (RRIFs)

RRIFs are extensions of RRSPs; RRSPs must be converted to RRIFs by age seventy-one. You are required to make minimum annual RRIF withdrawals (based on age) but can draw more than the minimum any time you wish. Like RRSPs, funds within an RRIF may be invested in stocks, bonds, GICs, ETFs, and other products without incurring tax, but withdrawals are treated as taxable income.

Locked-In Retirement Accounts (LIRAs) and Locked-In Retirement Savings Plans (LRSPs)

Meant to act like individual pension plans, LIRAs and LRSPs are retirement accounts designed to hold 'locked-in' funds for former members of employer pension plans. For example, if you worked for an employer that sponsored a pension plan and elected to take the value of your pension as a lump sum upon leaving your employer, you would have to deposit the funds in one of these plans, where it is locked in and not accessible to you until retirement age.

Once created, you cannot make further contributions to a LIRA or LRSP, and you may not withdraw funds until a specified age (typically ranging from age fifty-five to seventy-one), at which point annual withdrawals *must* commence. Like an RRSP, funds within a LIRA or LRSP may be invested in stocks, bonds, GICs, ETFs, and so on without incurring tax on any gains, but withdrawals are treated as taxable income.

RRSPs for
First-Time Homebuyers

RRSPs can be used as a tax-effective means of saving for a home down payment. You and your spouse can withdraw up to $25,000 each from RRSPs for this purpose. The rules are complicated, though, so do your research. For example, you must replace these funds in your RRSP over a number of years. For details, check out the CRA website.

2. No Thanks! Investments You Can Ignore

This book focuses on Simply Successful Investing through common stocks, bonds, GICs, and low-cost index ETFs while avoiding overpriced mutual funds. There are several other types of market investments that, in my view, should be approached with a high degree of caution or simply avoided altogether by the average Canadian investor.

Corporate Bonds

Corporate bonds generally offer coupons higher than government bonds because of greater perceived default risk. Default risk represents the possibility that the borrower fails to pay interest and repay principal when due as a result of bankruptcy or some other severe stress. There are two main categories within the corporate bond universe: 'investment grade' bonds, which are issued by financially stronger companies, and 'high yield' or 'junk' bonds issued by weaker companies. Both categories of corporate bonds are subject to significant market price declines—not just from increasing interest rates, but also from generally deteriorating economic conditions and any specific issues impacting the particular issuer. Owning corporate bonds through a broadly diversified index ETF can form part of any Simply Successful Investment approach, but directly buying individual corporate bond issues requires a level of sophistication beyond the average investor.

Preferred Shares

Preferreds were once a low-drama alternative to bonds for generating reliable investment income. Now, they're a top name on any ranking of wealth-destroying investments. ROB CARRICK, *THE GLOBE AND MAIL,* FEBRUARY 12, 2016

Would you buy an investment that has virtually no upside potential, unlimited downside potential, and under which the issuer has absolutely no legal obligation to either make any ongoing payments or ultimately pay you back your principal... ever? Canadian investors own about $60 billion of these beauties, which are otherwise known as preferred shares.

Preferred shares are very different from common shares; they behave more like high yield, low quality bonds. Here are some of the key attributes of preferred shares:

1. While bond issuers are legally bound to pay interest, preferred share issuers have no legal obligation to pay dividends. For example, CIBC is legally obliged to pay scheduled interest payments on GICs and deposits but must only pay preferred share dividends if declared by the board of directors. I'm not saying CIBC is unlikely to pay—Canadian banks and most other blue chip companies have a consistent record of declaring and paying preferred share dividends—I'm just saying there is no obligation.

2. Most bonds have a specified maturity date when the issuer is obliged to give investors their money back. Most preferred shares (including those with five-year dividend reset provisions) are 'perpetual,' which means investors never actually have the *legal right* to get their money back. However, issuers have the right, at regular intervals, to redeem preferred shares at the original issue price. Does that sound like a one-way street? It sure is. The issuer's right to redeem at the original price caps the value of preferred shares roughly around their original issue price, but the ability of the issuer to leave preferred shares outstanding in perpetuity means you have no downside protection.

3. To offset their shortcomings versus bonds, preferred shares offer (non-obligatory) dividend rates much higher than interest rates on bonds. And preferred dividends receive the same favourable tax treatment as common share dividends.

4. As implied by the earlier quote from Rob Carrick, for years many investors thought of preferred shares as sort of a safe, low-risk, high-yield sleepy hollow. During the 2008/2009 financial crisis, and again a couple of years ago, many preferred shares issued by blue chip companies including major banks and insurers suffered market value losses of 30–50 percent.

5. The great majority of new bond and common stock issues are purchased by large institutional investors. Average investors get very little if any access to these new issues. Not so with preferred shares. In fact, the great majority of preferred share new issues are purchased by individual investors, not because the issuer or Bay Street is doing anybody any favours, but because the majority of sophisticated institutional investors want no part of them.

Steer clear of preferred shares.

Mortgage Investments

There are a number of small, high-risk mortgage operators tempting investors with *potential* annual returns of 6–10 percent, or even more. Remember, if an investment sounds too good to be true, it probably is. These products are typically loaded with fees and offer very limited ability to get out early if you become uncomfortable or need your money. And when the economic downturns arrive (you know they will) these investments may experience serious, unrecoverable losses. Don't take the bait.

Gold

An ounce of gold would have set you back close to US$2,000 in January 1980. As of April 2018, the best price you could get for that same ounce of gold was around US$1,350. A US$2,000 investment in the S&P 500 index in January 1980 with dividends reinvested would be worth US$130,000 as of April 2018.

Enough said.

Bitcoin and Other Cryptocurrencies

I am pretty sure Bitcoin and the other new blockchain-based currencies will rocket higher and crash and burn. I just have no idea how often, when, and in which order! Cryptocurrencies are currently for speculators only.

3. Special FX

Investing outside of Canada introduces a foreign exchange (FX) risk, which is produced by changes in the Canadian dollar exchange rate versus the currency in which your investment is denominated (e.g., US dollars).

Figure A.1: Canadian/US Dollar Average Annual Exchange Rates[1]

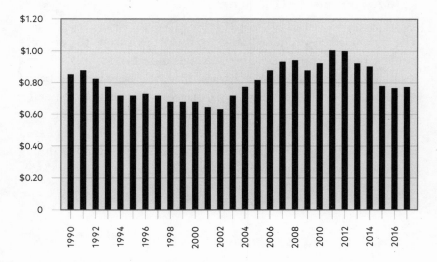

For example, buying US$10,000 worth of US stocks when the Canadian dollar is worth US$0.80 will cost you C$12,500. If the Canadian dollar increases in value to US$0.90, your US$10,000 in stocks will be worth only C$11,111.11. Conversely, if the Canadian dollar decreases in value to US$0.70, your US$10,000 in stocks will be worth C$14,285.71.

What strategies can be used to manage FX risk?

1. **Correlation:** stick to the major foreign currency that is the least volatile versus Canadian dollars; that is, US dollars.
2. **Clockwork:** simply ignore currency levels. Steadily invest in foreign markets over time to smooth the way in as you build your portfolio, and steadily sell down on the way out as you draw down funds during retirement.
3. **Hedge:** purchase 'currency hedged' ETFs, which track major US or global indexes but eliminate the effect of changes in Canadian dollar exchange rates, e.g., Vanguard's 'Canadian Dollar Hedged' S&P 500 Index ETF (VSP).

4. Mutual Fund T-REX Scores

The data used to produce Table 3.5 was drawn from the sources noted on the next page. The pre-fee rates of return assumed for the mutual funds listed in Table 3.5 are displayed here and are based on 6.5 percent for stock funds, 3.9 percent for bond funds, and a proportionately blended return for balanced funds based on their approximate stock/bond mix. These rates of return are based on Financial Planning Standards Council's (FPSC's) 2017 planning guidelines for Canadian stocks and bonds.

Table A.1: Mutual Fund Data

Source of Size, Type, Fee information	Assumed Rate of Return	Annual Fee
RBC Select Conservative Portfolio Fund Facts Feb 28, 2018	4.94%	1.84%
Investors Dividend C Fund Facts Jun 30, 2017	6.50%	2.80%
Fidelity Monthly Income Fund Facts Oct 27, 2017	4.91%	2.28%
TD Canadian Core Plus Bond Fund Facts Jul 27, 2017	3.90%	1.51%
Manulife Monthly High-Income B Fund Facts Feb 28, 2018	5.36%	2.29%
Scotia Canadian Dividend Fund A Fund Facts Feb 28, 2018	6.50%	1.73%
Sentry Canadian Income Fund A Fund Facts Feb 21, 2018	6.50%	2.34%
CI Signature Income & Growth A Fund Facts Feb 28, 2018	5.62%	2.41%
Mackenzie Income Fund A Fund Facts Sep 29, 2017	4.68%	1.89%
BMO SelectTrust Balanced A Fund Facts Apr 24, 2017	5.00%	2.50%
Trimark Fund A Fund Facts Nov 2, 2017	6.50%	2.70%
Desjardins Enhanced Bond C Fund Facts Jan 18, 2018	3.90%	1.70%
National Bank Bond Fund Facts May 12, 2017	3.90%	1.59%
Sun Life Granite Balanced A Fund Facts Mar 9 2018	5.54%	2.22%

Notes

Chapter 1

1. Ajay Khorana, Henri Servaes, and Peter Tufano, "Mutual Fund Fees around the World," HBS Finance Working Paper 901023, May 8, 2006.
2. "The Boiling Frog Story," May 16, 2011, www.wikipedia.org

Chapter 3

1. Canada Stock Channel, Compound Returns Calculator, www.canadastockchannel.com/compound-returns-calculator
2. TD Bank Group, "Share Price & Tools," www.td.com/investor-relations/ir-homepage/share-information/share-price-tools/investment-calculator.jsp
3. Tangerine Bank, "Many Canadian Investors Unaware of Fees They're Paying to Invest," press release, July 13, 2016, www.tangerine.ca
4. Government of Canada, Tax-Free Savings Accounts, "Contributions," www.canada.ca/en/revenue-agency/services/tax/individuals/topics/tax-free-savings-account/contributions
5. Inflation.eu, www.inflation.eu

Chapter 4

1. BMO Harris Bank television commercial, posted on YouTube, "BMO Harris Bank sports commercial," www.youtube.com/watch?v=FUIAa6DWI00

Chapter 5

1. Investopedia, www.investopedia.com/terms/m/morningstarriskrating.asp
2. Juhani T. Linnainmaa, Brian T. Melzer, and Alessandro Previtero, "The Misguided Beliefs of Financial Advisors," Working Paper, 2017.
3. Morningstar, www.morningstar.ca

Chapter 7

1. Dimensional Returns 2.0, software, http://dimensional-returns.software.
   informer.com/2.0/
2. Moneychimp calculator, "Compound Annual Growth Rate (Annualized
   Return)," www.moneychimp.com/features/market_cagr.htm
3. Canadian ETF Association (CETFA), www.cetfa.ca
4. IFIC, www.ific.ca
5. Blackrock, www.blackrock.com/ca/individual/en/products/239832/
   ishares-sptsx-60-index-etf
6. Vanguard, www.vanguardcanada.ca/individual/indv/en/product.html#/
   fundDetail/etf/portId=9563/assetCode=equity/?overview

Chapter 8

1. Morningstar, http://quote.morningstar.ca/quicktakes/Fund/f_ca.aspx?
   t=F0CAN05M27&culture=en-CA&region=CAN
2. RBC Select Conservative Portfolio Fund Facts, February 28, 2018.

Chapter 9

1. www.marketwired.com/press-release/blackrock-2015-global-investor-
   pulse-survey-canadians-place-high-priority-on-saving-2067299.htm

Chapter 10

1. Retirement Readiness Calculator, in Rob Carrick and Michael Pereira,
   "Ready for Retirement? Find out Your Replacement Ratio," *The Globe
   and Mail*, February 18, 2016, updated February 13, 2018.
2. Rob Carrick, "A Rule for Funding Golden Years," *The Globe and Mail*,
   June 4, 2009, updated March 26, 2017, www.theglobeandmail.com/
   globe-investor/investment-ideas/a-rule-for-funding-golden-years/
   article786910/
3. TD Bank Group, TD Retirement Calculator, www.tdcanadatrust.com/
   products-services/investing/retirement-savings-calculator/
4. Government of Canada, Benefits, "Canadian Retirement Income
   Calculator," www.canada.ca/en/services/benefits/publicpensions/
   cpp/retirement-income-calculator.html

Appendix

1. OFX, Yearly Average Rates, "Historical Exchange Rates," www.ofx.com/
   en-ca/forex-news/historical-exchange-rates/yearly-average-rates/

Acknowledgements

THANKS TO Jesse Finkelstein and the team at Page Two Strategies for your support and guidance throughout the process of bringing this book from concept to publication. Thanks also to my diligent and insightful editor, Karen Milner.

To Alexander Younger and the talented team at Design Lab, thank you for creating a great website for me.

I am very grateful to my many friends and colleagues who took the time to review and comment on various aspects of *Beat the Bank*. Your contributions were essential to the development of the book.

I greatly appreciate the support of the small band of investor advocates I have come to know over the past couple of years. Your efforts on behalf of millions of Canadian investors do not get the recognition they deserve, but you are making a difference! I have learned a great deal from you.

I would also like to thank the personal finance authors, columnists, and educators who have kindly shared their experiences and offered encouragement along the way. And sincere thanks to the notable individuals who took the time to read *Beat the Bank* and provide wonderful endorsements.

Finally, I must offer very special thanks to my wife, Alyson, and my entire family. Your encouragement, support, ideas, and patience provided me with the foundation to see this project through. And to my sister, Mary, thanks for the inspiration to get me started!

More about
Beat the Bank

G O TO WWW.LARRYBATES.CA for Simply Successful Investing resources, insights, updates, and links to other helpful websites. You will also be able to connect with a community of other investors and learn about their Simply Successful Investing journeys.

And please sign up to my *Beat the Bank* newsletter.

You can also follow me on Twitter, LinkedIn, and Facebook.

Let me know what you think about *Beat the Bank*. I can be reached through my website or at larry@larrybates.ca.

If you enjoyed *Beat the Bank* and believe the book can help others achieve better investment outcomes, please tell your family and friends! Also, please consider leaving a review of *Beat the Bank* on www.amazon.ca and www.indigo.ca.

Bulk Sales

Beat the Bank is available for bulk purchase at a discount. For more information, contact me at larry@larrybates.ca.

About the Author

———

LARRY BATES IS a former banker turned investor advocate, author, investment coach, and speaker. He currently serves as a Member of the Investor Advisory Panel of the Ontario Securities Commission and as an Ambassador of the Transparency Task Force.

Larry was raised in the Maritimes and earned a business degree from Dalhousie University. Upon graduation from Dal, and after failing to make it past the first interview with the federal public service—his top job choice—Larry set off on a thirty-five-year banking career with several prominent institutions in Halifax, Toronto, and London, England, including as Global Head of Debt Capital Markets for RBC. Over the course of his career, Larry both collaborated with and advised many of the world's most sophisticated investors and financial institutions.

Currently residing with his wife Alyson in Toronto, Larry enjoys spending time with his adult children, playing third base on his soft-ball team, and occasionally breaking ninety on the golf course.

Larry believes Canadians can retire better and, if desired, sooner through Simply Successful Investing. For more about Larry, go to www.larrybates.ca.